Dr. Oma

CHOSEN DAUGHTERS

Wings like a Dove, *by Christine Farenhorst*

Dr. Oma, *by Ethel Herr*

Dr. Oma

THE HEALING WISDOM OF
COUNTESS JULIANA VON STOLBERG

ETHEL HERR

P&R
PUBLISHING
P.O. BOX 817 • PHILLIPSBURG • NEW JERSEY 08865-0817

Unless otherwise indicated, Scripture quotations are from the NEW AMERICAN STAN-DARD BIBLE®. Copyright © 1960, 1962, 1963, 1968, 1971, 1972, 1973, 1975, 1977, 1995 by The Lockman Foundation. Used by permission.

Page design by Dawn Premako
Typesetting by Lakeside Design Plus
Map by Stephen Mitchell

Printed in the United States of America

ISBN-10: 0-87552-641-1
ISBN-13: 978-0-87552-641-6

To Lauren
My special granddaughter,
who reminds me often what it was like to be young.
Thank you for brainstorming with me about Juliana and Maria.
I love you.

To Ellen
Friend, writing partner, editor *par excellence*.
Thank you for falling in love with Juliana and Maria,
for pouring yourself into this project
and touching it with the sparkle
of your wit, eloquence, and remarkable sense about people.

N

SCOTLAND

North
Sea

NORWAY

SWEDEN

IRELAND

DENMARK

ENGLAND

NETHERLANDS

Atlantic
Ocean

Breda

HOLY
ROMAN
EMPIRE

Wernigerode

Brussels

Wittenburg

Dillenburg

Stolberg

Worms

Konigstein

FRANCE

SWITZERLAND

HUNGARY

OTTOMAN
EMPIRE

PORTUGAL

SPAIN

ITALY

Rome

NORTH AFRICA

Mediterranean
Sea

CONTENTS

ACKNOWLEDGMENTS

For more years than most of my readers have even been alive, I've loved Juliana von Stolberg. I met her in an old history book with no pictures. But the story of her life made me want to meet her in person—and to introduce her to the whole world.

Several years later, I visited the Royal Dutch Archives in The Hague, Netherlands. I'd had to get a letter of permission from Queen Beatrix herself in order to be allowed into this wonderful place. My heart beat with great excitement as I entered the impressive old building. I loved the atmosphere created by its dark wood paneled walls, echoing floors, and miles and miles of shelves. The man who ran the archive gave me a list of things I could look at. I chose the items I wanted, and he brought them to me.

The high point for me came when he brought me a bundle of old, yellowed letters. There, on each envelope, I could see the ink letters, scrawled by the hand of Juliana von Stolberg four hundred years before. The fragile envelopes still had blobs of sealing wax affixed to them to keep them closed. I held them all like delicate jewels and felt the tears coming to my eyes. In that incredible moment of wonder, I felt as if I was in the physical presence of this dear old woman. That's when my heart knew what my head had been telling me for years—Juliana von Stolberg was a real live woman.

I felt her presence, too, when I stood on the hill at Dillenburg and looked out across the field where once she grew and harvested her herbs. The castle she called home is gone now, but some of the old walls remain down at the foot of the hill. I heard the beautiful bell ring out in the church on the side of the hill where she now lies buried, and knew she used to listen to that exact same sound many times each day of her busy life.

Then I came home and read all the books about her I could find. What a wonderful "beloved mother of us all" she was!

When Melissa Craig asked me to write Juliana's story for you, I was absolutely delighted. Eagerly, I enlisted the help of friends and family. My granddaughter, Lauren Herr, told me what a girl her age would like and not like. My dear friend, Ellen Cohen, brainstormed ideas with me, then read every word I wrote, made lots of corrections and suggestions, and kept telling me what a wonderful story it was. A group of girls from my church—Kristen and Amy Hahn and Christy de Villiers—along with their mothers, read the manuscript and gave me helpful suggestions. So did my schoolteacher friend, Cathy Cooper, and two of her former students, Brenna Stanton and Kristine Cabugao.

I thank these, along with all the others who worked on the team and made *Dr. Oma: The Healing Wisdom of Countess Juliana von Stolberg* happen as a book!

- Alice Funkhouser, my dear mother, who taught me how to be a godly woman and spent many hours listening to the stories of Juliana as I learned them.

- John Motley, who, more than a century ago, wrote that old dusty book, where I first read about Juliana.
- Her Majesty, Queen Beatrix, Juliana's descendent on the Dutch throne, who let me use her archives.
- Mr. Woelderink, the royal archive director, who put Juliana's letters in my hands.
- Dr. Lewis Spitz, who encouraged me years ago to write Juliana's story.
- Ranelda Hunsicker and Melissa Craig, who asked me to write this book, then edited it and guided the process.
- Each one of you as you read and enjoy and learn godliness from Juliana von Stolberg.

Many thanks to you all!
Ethel Herr

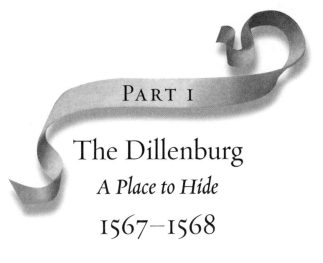

PART I

The Dillenburg
A Place to Hide
1567–1568

Lavender:

Lavender is almost wholly spent with us, for to perfume linen, apparel, gloves and leather and the dryed flowers to comfort and dry up the moisture of a cold braine. —JOHN PARKINSON

A reminder of your first herbal lesson. It speaks to you of devotion and virtue—two things you will always need if you are to become a true noble-woman. It will cheer you on a gray day, with its purple color, and its aroma will add beauty to the room where you sleep. —OMA

I

THE SURPRISE VISIT

APRIL 1567

On a night that gave no reason to be different from any other, Maria prepared herself by lamplight to climb into her big bed with the hanging curtains, brocade spreads, and huge pillows. Toske, her attendant, had just removed the girl's headdress and ribbons and loosened her honey-colored hair from its carefully plaited bun. Maria shook her head, and she and Toske laughed together. How she loved it when her hair fell in silky cascades around her shoulders. It made her feel like a princess—which she almost was.

She was gathering up the long flowing skirt of her sleeping gown and padding across the floor toward her bed, when unexpectedly the huge old wooden doors of her apartment opened. Startled, Maria looked up to see her mistress, Duchess Margaretha of Parma, accompanied by her highest ranking lady-in-waiting.

Maria sucked in her breath. What could this mean?

She watched the noble woman walk through the room with its high ceilings and dark paneled walls toward her. Each step, each movement reminded Maria that this straight, severe woman with the pearls at her neck and sprinkled in the hair piled atop her head was the lady of this castle. Regent of the Provinces, so Maria had been taught. She didn't much understand what that all meant. It was enough that she was an important woman. Maria knew how fortunate she was to be in training to become one of the duchess's ladies-in-waiting.

Two years ago, when she was nine years old, Maria's father, Willem van Oranje, had brought her here to live with, learn from, and attend to Duchess Margaretha in the royal court of Brussels. Often the girl went off to her apartment to learn how to prepare the duchess's bath or fix her hair or wait on any one of her other many needs. But the royal lady never came here to her room.

Maria held her skirt and hands in the precise way she had been instructed, and curtsied before the woman.

"G-good evening, Your Highness," she stammered.

The royal visitor nodded to acknowledge the show of respect. She stood staring down at Maria, arms folded, a permanent scowl pressed into her forehead.

She forced a half-smile at Maria and spoke with a frighteningly drippy sweetness. "Your father has sent for you."

"My father?" Maria gasped.

"Yes, child. He is taking you to the Dillenburg—to his mother, your Oma, Countess Juliana von Stolberg."

"Going to see Oma?" Anticipation leaped inside Maria, and she felt as if she would explode with happiness at the thought.

Nothing brought her so much joy as being with her grandmother. Maria had never known her own mother, only Oma. She did not come often to visit, but when she did, she played games with Maria and her brother, Philips Willem. Often Oma read and sang songs to them and held them close. Ah, yes, to see Oma with her always-smiling mouth and sparkling eyes—that would be a treat above all treats!

But the duchess no longer smiled. "Your father says the countess is not well," she said.

Maria gasped again. Her precious Oma, the healer lady who spent her life dispensing potions and salves to bring life to others—not well?

Margaretha tilted her head slightly toward the girl. Maria searched her eyes but found no comfort there. "She is calling for you. She wants to see you one more time before she dies."

"Before she dies? Oh no! She cannot be that ill." Maria covered her mouth with her hands and swallowed down the panicky feeling that rose in her throat.

It seemed to her the woman did not move for a long time. Oh! The icy stab in those dark, fearsome eyes! They stared a hole through to her inner being. Maria backed away from her visitor slowly, one step at a time, until she sat perched on the edge of her bed.

The duchess began pacing back and forth around the big four-poster bed, arms still folded, smiles all gone. Like an animal caught in a cage, Maria pulled her feet up, tucking them in under her nightdress, hugging her legs. A chill ran through her entire body, and she leaned back against her pillows.

Margaretha spoke again. "That's what your father says in his message to me. He has asked me to prepare you to leave for Breda tomorrow. From there, you go to the Dillenburg."

"Oh, then I will see my brother!" Maria's face grew suddenly warm and her heart beat so fast, she could feel its steady thumping. How she loved Philips Willem! Up until she had come here to live in the court in Brussels, he had been her constant friend and playmate. Only fourteen months older than she, he'd always been there. Living here in this place without him had left her often lonely. She had no friend to replace him.

But Margaretha was staring at her with unfeeling eyes. "I didn't say your brother was going with you," she said, a cold edge to her harsh voice.

"Bu . . . but, Your Grace," Maria stammered, "surely if Oma is dying, she will want to see Philips Willem as well."

The regal woman cleared her throat, and walked back and forth in half-circles around the foot of the bed. Then, with arms folded tightly across her waist, she said icily, "Your brother is a man now, committed to his education at the University of Leuven. He cannot be running off to visit an ailing grandmother. Your father will take you, and your stepmother will go along, with her young child." She paused and Maria watched a smirky half-smile spread across the severe face of the woman looking down on her.

Father's wife, Anna, was going? Why? Anna hated Oma! Maria's flesh turned cold and goosey at the thought. Anna, that strange wild woman who acted more like some fearsome animal than anybody's stepmother! Maria remembered well the scary years when she and Philips Willem lived with Father and his new wife in the big castle in Breda—all too well, she remembered—and shuddered.

At the thought of Anna going along with them, Maria's mind swarmed with memories of Anna's terrorizing the entire household with her drinking bouts, her loud angry shouts, and nasty words. And when Father was gone on a trip, she often seemed to have visits from strange men in her apartment. How many nights Philips Willem had hugged Maria and helped her fears to go away. How could she endure Anna without her brother close by? Memories of Mad Anna had given her nightmares that persisted long after she'd come here, where Father had brought her to be safe from her stepmother's mad rampages. A jumble of thoughts tormented the girl.

Minutes ago, she had been happily ready to fall into bed for a good night's rest. Now suddenly she had many reasons to be sad and fearful of tomorrow.

Yes, it made her glad to know that she was going to see her father! How she missed him! Handsome, strong, witty, and kind; she was proud to be his daughter! He'd only been here to see her a few times since she came two years ago. But always he'd had an embrace and a kiss for her. Even at eleven years, she knew she could expect the warmth of his strong arms holding her close.

But Philips Willem was not coming—and Oma was dying! No, no! She shook her head in protest. It had to be a mistake!

Why had Margaretha of Parma come here in person tonight to tell her all this?

To Maria, the duchess was a great mystery! On one hand, she seemed fond of telling Maria that she cared for her as she would a daughter. It was true that she gave her all the comforts of life a girl could ask for—beautiful clothes, a fine room, the opportunity to serve her noble highness. But Maria felt no warmth from her.

Further, Maria had a few times overheard Margaretha talking about Father Willem with an angry tone of voice and words to match. But then, she did this with all the men who came and went at court, not just Father. She often went into long, dark pouting spells after she'd argued with any of the important men—or when she got a letter from her brother, King Philip. He lived far away in Spain. Everybody in the court talked about Margaretha's sullen spells and scurried out of her way whenever she acted strange. Always, Maria saw something frightening in her eyes. Cold. Yes, that was it. Even when it seemed she intended them to look warm.

Maria looked up to see the woman moving toward the bed, coming deliberately forward and sitting beside her—not quite close enough to touch her. Maria drew her knees a bit tighter to her chest.

"Before you leave," the duchess began in her usual distant tone and manner, "I want to remind you of the three most important things I've tried to teach you since you came here to live. I want to know you have learned them well, before I let you go away."

"But I will be back soon," Maria interrupted, not quite asking a question, not quite making a statement.

The duchess cleared her throat and adjusted the pearls hanging around the neck of her heavy brocade bodice. "Of course you will be back, my child. But where you are going, you will meet with well-meaning but deluded persons who will tempt you to forget the lessons I have taught you. For your own protection you must never forget." She looked straight at Maria again and repeated, "Never!" She paused, and Maria sat frozen in her place. "Do you understand?"

Why must her eyes feel so like sharp daggers piercing clear to Maria's soul? She mumbled, "Yes, Your Highness. I understand."

"Very well, then. First, if you would be safe in this unfriendly world, understand that your stepmother, Anna, grew up reading the Protestant Bible. Avoid that book, or you too, may grow as mad as Anna—or worse." She stopped, then added, "Only heretics read the Protestant Bible! Do you understand what I'm telling you?"

Whatever was a heretic? Maria wondered. She'd heard the word spoken in horror, but had been too afraid to ask. One thing she did know. Heretics were wicked people, and when caught, they were cast into prison or put to death in public places. Why reading the Bible should be such a wicked thing to do, Maria could not imagine. But then, she'd never seen a Bible herself or heard anyone read from such a book. She had no intention of looking for one, especially if it had caused Anna to go mad!

Too frightened by the fierce tone of Margaretha's voice to admit she did not understand, Maria mumbled again. "Yes, Your Highness."

"Now, second," Duchess Margaretha went on, in an important tone. "If you should be so unfortunate as to marry a heretic husband, know this: he would threaten everything you have learned that has made you noble and gentle. And further, your children—if, indeed, you were to have children—would inherit the curse that stains him."

Maria stared in disbelief. Marriage? The duchess, sensing her distress began again, quickly, "I can see that you think you are too young to talk of marriage. But I assure you, you are more lucky than you know. When I was twelve years old—only one year older than you are now—my father gave me in marriage to a twenty-seven-year-old drunkard and gambler." She paused for effect and smiled one of those strange distant smiles that never made Maria feel warm. "Of course, as long as you're with me, child, you will not have to worry about such things! I will watch out for you. Do you understand?"

Maria wriggled in her place, feeling the woman suddenly too close. "Yes, Your Highness," she said at last. Her words felt dry in her throat. When would this questioning end?

Margaretha pointed a stick-like finger at her. "And, this last is especially important. DO NOT forget it!" Maria drew back into her pillows, as the woman's voice rose to nearly a shout. "Remember! All heretics are devious demons. No matter how sweet they appear on the surface, nor how long that sweetness lasts, they are leading you into demonic places. Whether it be the kitchen cook or your dearest family member, you must guard yourself. Do not let anyone get too close."

Maria trembled. Surely she wouldn't meet any of these kinds of people at the Dillenburg. Anna might be a heretic, but surely, no one else was—and everyone ignored the mad woman. Margaretha glared at her. Clearly, she waited for some kind of response.

"Yes, Your Highness."

"Very well, then, fair little lady." Margaretha seemed to soften slightly. "You will be safe, if you remember these things, and keep them close to your heart. When you return to me, I shall keep you safe, right here beside me. When the time comes, I shall find you a kind and fitting husband, and all will go well with you."

Margaretha of Parma smiled and laid a hand ever so briefly on Maria's shoulder. "Now, sleep well. My maids have packed your things. and all is in readiness for your journey. You must rest and prepare yourself for the long day that lies before you."

The stately woman rose and strode to the door. Her attendant opened it and ushered her out. Every burning lamp in the apartment flickered with the movement and set strange shadow forms dancing across the walls and into Maria's confused mind. When Maria's attendants had settled her into bed, Toske whispered into the hair that fell across her ear, "Fear not, my child. I shall go with you."

"Thank you, Toske, thank you, " Maria whispered back, then clung tightly to the old lady's neck.

All Maria's life, this plump and pleasant Toske had tucked her into bed at night. She was the closest thing to a mother Maria had ever known. Her own mother died when she was two years old, or so Toske had told her. Tonight, Maria wanted to pull the woman into bed beside her. How she needed to feel someone close! But it could not happen—at court, of all places. Maria was, after all, the daughter of a nobleman. Toske, but a servant woman. Other attendants—people from the court—hovered nearby, with hawk's eyes to see whenever something was not done according to the rules.

Maria lay alone in her big bed for long hours, her thoughts much too confused to allow her to sleep. How she yearned to see Father and Oma and Philips Willem!

Oh, my dear brother. Her mind began composing a letter to him. *You promised me, when we were parted, that you would love me always and lend me a warm shoulder on which to weep. I shall ask Father to take you with us to the Dillenburg. I cannot face a Mad Anna and a dying Oma without you beside me. Oh, my dearest friend, Philips Willem . . .*

At last she fell asleep with her brother's name on her lips and moisture on her cheeks. Good dreams about Oma and Father and scary nightmares about Anna and Bibles—and Duchess Margaretha—chased each other in dizzy circles until at last daybreak came, to bring her relief.

2

THE RUBY NECKLACE

APRIL 1567

The day was gray when Maria arrived home in Breda. How eager she was to see her father, to be home again, even if it was only for a few days! The old castle on the edge of the city had been home to her all her life until just two years ago. Yet how could it feel right without Philips Willem? And what had happened to Oma? Would she live till they arrived?

Maria stepped down from the carriage into cool, damp afternoon air on the arm of her coachman, then entered through the old wooden gate and found herself immediately in her father's arms.

"Oh, Father," she cried out and nestled her face into his uniform.

"You grow into such a fine lady," he said, and his voice sent shivers of delight straight to her heart. "I am filled with joy to have you under my roof once more."

He took her shoulders in his big hands and held her where he could look into her eyes. She surveyed his handsome face and sharp pointed beard. They exchanged smiles. Then, Maria turned sober and asked, "Is Oma so very ill, Father?"

Father Willem said nothing for a long while, just stood there holding her in his arms. At last, he said simply, "When we arrive in the Dillenburg, we shall see . . ."

"You think she will die soon?"

He shrugged his big shoulders with the padded jacket and golden chains and said, "In God's good time—not one minute sooner or later."

"She is dreadfully ill, then?" Maria felt a panic rising inside.

In a calm manner that sometimes made her feel safe, but in times like this made her more fearful than ever, he answered, "We shall see, but we go to her just as soon as we can put all in readiness."

Maria followed him into the living apartment. Visions of a dying Oma flooded her mind, and she felt so alone. If only her brother were here to talk with! He could always make her feel better.

She tugged at her father's hand and said, "But Father, what of Philips Willem? Please, may he go along with us?"

Father Willem sighed. "Not now. Maybe later he can join us."

"Oh, Father, I miss him so much. I miss . . . just talking to him."

Father put his hands behind his back and stared at the floor as they walked. Maria heard sadness in his voice, felt it in the air around them. "These are not easy times for a Prince of Oranje or for his family," he said, and, as always, she felt as if he held some deep, sad secrets from her.

"But why can Philips Willem not go with us?" she insisted.

Father opened the door into the apartment, then said simply, "He is a man now, my child. Duty must come first. Oma will understand, and so must we."

From that point on, he spoke of other things and sent her to her room to rest from her long journey. She threw herself on the bed and cried until she fell asleep with loneliness and exhaustion.

When she awoke, Toske was jiggling her shoulder and calling, "Wake up, my lady, the dinner bell is sounding."

Her eyes felt puffy and warm, and her cheeks were streaked with dried tears. She pulled herself up, splashed water on her face, and tried to look pleasant as she followed Toske to the dining room.

How everything had changed! Surely she was not really walking through the halls of her childhood home. This must be a strange dream. The once-colorful walls were bare and many of the floors as well. Tapestries and paintings, tables and chairs—where had they gone? Even her bedroom held nothing more than the basic covers and pillows she would need to keep her warm in her sleep.

For the next few days, Maria wandered around the old castle in a fog. Where were all those precious things she'd loved to look at as a child? Vases, silver candlesticks, lamps, tapestries, carved wooden furniture, and big padded chairs—where had they gone? The halls echoed with busy steps. Servants seemed happy to see her, but she saw sadness in their eyes and heard it in their voices.

When at last she asked her Toske what was happening, the older woman shook her head and said, "Ask no more questions, child. Soon we leave to go to the Dillenburg."

"But where have all the treasures gone?"

Toske repeated her words, "I told you to ask no more questions, child. Soon we leave for the Dillenburg." She paused, laid a gentle hand on Maria's shoulder, then added, "There it will all be made plain."

Most disturbing of all, the empty halls seemed, day after day, to echo with the ugly sounds of Anna's voice:

"I will not go!" the mad woman screamed, followed by long strings of foul and hateful words, most often directed at Father Willem.

"How can you wrench me from this beautiful place where I am the lady?" she shrieked over and over. "I hate you, I hate you, I hate you!"

Again and again, Maria heard it and shivered and wrapped herself in her cloak. Often she fled to the garden of hedgerow shrubbery where she and Philips Willem had spent so many delightful hours chasing after each other, brushing their clothes against the fragrant herbs. If only she could turn back the clock, bring back Philips Willem, get rid of Anna, and know that Oma would be well and strong forever!

Instead, she heard echoes in her mind of Duchess Margaretha's warnings against Protestant husbands, a Protestant Bible, and Protestant heretics. She listened to the rantings of her mad Protestant stepmother and wondered what it was all about.

Without your brother, she told herself, as she stood looking out over the garden, *you will need to call up every ounce of courage you can find lodged in your heart.* She sighed and answered herself with as big a voice as she could muster, "I shall try."

At last the morning came when all the coaches had been loaded. People and horses formed into a huge caravan and prepared to move out. Maria knew it was not uncommon to take along many servants on a visit to relatives. But she still wondered about the furnishings. Why had they disappeared? Were they packed away to be carried along on this visit of no more than a few weeks?

Puzzled, she watched Father Willem move about between little knots of people. As lord of the castle, he gave final words of instruction to the servants staying behind, about what to do in his absence.

How tired he looks, Maria thought. *Tired and unhappy and worried! I think he does not want to go.*

As Maria waited for one of the servants to help her mount the horse she was going to ride, from a distance the loud clopping of horses' hooves across the cobblestones reached her ears. Everyone gathered in front of the castle stable looked up, startled to see a small group of mounted horsemen rapidly approaching. Maria watched her father walk to greet them and held her breath.

The men were dismounting now. She saw that one of them was shorter than all the rest. Father moved quickly toward him and embraced him with apparent enthusiasm.

Who is it? Maria crept closer until she could see the answer to her own question. It was no grown man, but . . . *Can it be? No, it cannot . . . but it is!*

"Philips Willem!" she cried out and dashed toward him.

How her beloved brother had changed over the two years that he had been gone from her! Taller now, dressed like a prince, he had lost some of his childlike appearance, and he did not smile even when she was sure he had seen her.

Maria's heart beat wildly. Was he still her friend? Would he chase her through the hedgerow garden if they had a chance? Or would he walk away and pretend to be a man with more important things to do? For what seemed a year, she waited while he and Father Willem talked.

At last, Father Willem stepped back and beckoned her forward. Philips Willem smiled a faint smile at her.

"Maria, my dear sister," he said in a way that made him feel far away.

She came close and reached her hand toward him. He took it in his own and squeezed it hard.

"Oh, Philips Willem," she said, trying hard not to sound too eager, though her heart had never been more so. "Are you going with us?"

"No, my sister," he said, his voice a mixture of coolness and a sort of excitement he seemed not to be able to show her. He dropped her hand and stood straight before her. "I am a man now. I must go back to school and learn my lessons and prepare for my life as a prince."

"Can you not even come to the Dillenburg for a short visit?" Maria felt her heart flutter and her hands grow sticky.

"Someday, perhaps, but not now," he answered.

If only they could have one hour together to run through the hedgerows and talk the way they'd always talked. So much she wanted to tell him, so many questions she wanted to ask! Did he know about Oma? What did he know about the empty walls and rooms in the old castle they were leaving? She opened her mouth to ask, but nothing came out.

All too soon Father Willem said, "We must be on our way, and you must return to your studies. I will come to you as soon as I am able. Honor your father and the memory of your mother by learning your lessons well. The days we face are difficult and dangerous, but our God is with us. My mother has told me so often. Heed her words—and all of mine."

Then they embraced, and Father turned to talk to the men who'd come with the boy. Philips Willem reached out to embrace Maria. For one short moment, she felt the joy and the wonder of still having her dear brother right here with her. She savored it much as she would a piece of candy. She gave him an extra squeeze, and he did the same to her. How could she let him go?

Quickly the moment passed. Father stepped forward, and they exchanged "good-byes" all around. Philips Willem climbed up onto his horse, taking the reins in hand. Maria watched as if looking at some dream from afar. Just when she thought she could not bear to see him leave, he motioned her to come close.

She moved to his side and looked up into his smiling eyes. He reached his hand into his doublet, then extended it to her.

"Here," he said. "Take this. It is for you."

She lifted her hand and let him place a tiny hard object in her open palm. He folded her fingers over it in a tight fist.

"I brought it for you," he said, sounding like the little boy she'd played with. "Keep it, and remember me."

Then, as quickly as the retinue of horsemen had arrived, they turned and rode off across the bridge and down the cobbled streets of the ancient city of Breda.

Maria watched them until the last little cloud of dust had disappeared from sight. Then carefully she opened her palm. Nestled there, she found a cut gemstone, attached to a slender golden chain. Bright ruby red, the jewel sparkled in the daylight. She stared in wonder.

"It's beautiful!" she whispered. "Thank you, Philips Willem. I shall wear it always beneath my clothes." Then lifting her eyes toward the horizon, she sent her words off into the wind toward the boy who was already out of sight.

A single warm soft tear fell into her hand, baptizing the stone with a unique combination of joy and sorrow.

Then she realized that Father Willem was calling his caravan to order. Maria hated to leave this magical spot, but she had to let a servant help her into the sidesaddle atop her horse. In a daze of emotion she felt her body being carried along with the long caravan moving off into the uncertainty of the future. She clutched the new gem on its chain as if her survival depended on keeping it. All day, she savored the memories of those few precious moments with Philips Willem—and struggled with fears of all that lay ahead.

3

A STORM AT THE DILLENBURG

At the end of the evening meal, Maria's plate sat empty on the table. It should be time for everyone to leave the dining hall. But that was not the way things were done in the old castle beside the Dill River in Germany Maids stopped scurrying about, and everyone grew silent at their places. Onkel Jan, lord of the Dillenburg, stepped up to the lectern desk in the corner of the massive hall. With wide hands, he smoothed his jacket over a paunchy belly, then looked down over his sharp little nose, past the trim, pointed beard, to a large book lying on the desk before him. He cleared his throat and began to read in a loud monotonous voice:

Trust in the Lord and do good;
Dwell in the land and meditate on the faithfulness of your God.

Maria squirmed. She knew well that the book Onkel Jan read from was a Bible—a German Bible. But was it a Protestant Bible? The kind Duchess Margaretha had warned her about? She had not dared to ask since she arrived here with her father two days ago.

Nothing else had gone as the duchess had told her it would on this journey, either. Back in Breda, she had suspected that they were not coming to the Dillenburg with all of their 150 servants and precious belongings just for a short visit. Also, she'd expected to find her grandmother in bed, too weak to breathe freely or smile. Instead Oma was the first to greet them at the castle gates. She looked and acted as strong and as well as ever, hugging Maria tight and long. Besides, no one—not even Maria's father—had mentioned any illness. Not once. Were they hiding something from her? She shook her head and wondered.

So, what about the duchess's warnings about the dangers of the Bible? Were they any more true than the story of Oma's illness? Everybody was nice enough to her, just like Margaretha had said they would be. How long would it be before the demons appeared?

Maria closed her ears to the Scripture reading as best she could and looked around the room. These people didn't look to her like heretics. Of course, the duchess had not told her what heretics looked like—just that they would deceive her. "No matter how sweet they appear"—those were the royal lady's words. So how could she know? Anna was mad and possibly a heretic, for all Maria knew, but even she appeared to fall asleep every time Onkel Jan read from his book.

Her mind wandered back to the big voice from the corner. "Rest in the Lord," she heard. "Wait patiently for Him; fret not yourself." Whatever did that mean? Was she fretting because she worried about these Bible readings that she must endure at five meals every day? He read from the Bible both before and after every meal! With each reading, her uneasiness grew.

Margaretha of Parma's shrill voice sounded in her memory now, drowning out all else around her: "Avoid that book, or you too, may grow to be like Anna—or worse."

Over and over, the words ran in her mind. She must get away from these sweet-appearing people and their strange Bible. But how? Father Willem would stop her if she left the room. If only Philips Willem were here. He would know what to do. But he was far, far away. She had to save herself!

Onkel Jan was closing the big book and bowing his head now! Ah, that was it! Everyone in the room bowed their heads and closed their eyes and Onkel Jan began to pray in a loud voice, "Oh Thou Almighty and gracious God, hear our prayers this day . . ." Maria did not look around her any more. As quietly and quickly as possible, she got up and moved across the room, grabbing her cloak as she went. She shoved open the unbolted door and stepped through into a misty spring evening. Never looking back, she ran out across the courtyard, down the maze of long corridors and archways that connected the many castle buildings, and out onto the road that led away from the castle and down the hill toward the village.

Where was she going? Where could she hide? She had no idea! But she must leave the demons behind! A shower of fine raindrops was falling on her head and her cloak and making little muddy puddles for her shoes to splash in. She pulled the hood up over her head and continued running, sometimes slipping on the wet stones.

Halfway down the hill, she spied a well-worn pathway leading off to a hedged enclosure. Could that be the famous herb garden she'd been told about? She remembered her father's sisters, Tante Juliana and Tante Magdalena, who had lived with them in Breda years ago, before Maria went to live at the court in Brussels. Often they mentioned this garden and all the marvelous cures Oma created from its leaves and roots and fruits.

She had dreamed that she would one day come here and see this wondrous place and learn its healing secrets. But for right now, with the rain beating down on her, it was enough to hope that she might at least find shelter from the pelting rain, there, under a tree. She desperately needed a refuge where she could think and plan what to do next.

Her skirts brushed against little clumps of weeds and field grasses as she ran down the path. At last she entered through an arbor of greenery into an enclosure filled with plants of all sorts. The rain seemed to release a hundred fragrances at once. They beckoned to the frightened girl, and she made her way through them till she came to a simple stone bench beneath a huge linden tree. It spread out its arms to offer a little protection from the now heavy rain.

She swiped at the bench with her hand, to rid it of the pool of water that had collected. Thankful for the thick absorbent layers her skirts placed between her and the bench, she sat, then put her head in her hands, rested her elbows on her legs, and wished her mind would slow down.

What could Maria believe?

She reached up and fingered the necklace Philips Willem had given to her. It gave her the feeling that he was there with her.

"Is Oma dying or not?" she asked aloud, hoping to hear his voice with an answer.

After all, what was so special about being here at the Dillenburg? Mad Anna had done nothing but rant and rave and scream and howl since they left Breda. She obviously did not want to be here and was making life miserable for the entire household.

And those continual Bible readings!

"Oh, Philips Willem, tell me. You know so many things, and now, you're so grown up! Will these Bible readings make me mad like Anna? The duchess said they would. Did she lie to me?"

She heard no answer. Only the sound of heavy rain fell on her ears. How could she ever learn the truth? Father seemed so sad and worried that she did not dare to ask him even a single question. And Oma? She was far too busy helping everyone get settled and trying to keep Anna happy to have time for Maria.

Dear Toske, who always spoke calm words and whom Maria trusted more than anyone else, seemed to have no answers for her. Maria felt more alone now than she had felt that last night in Brussels. If she couldn't see the danger, how could she protect herself?

"Almighty God, hear my prayers indeed!" Could God hear her if she prayed out here in this storm?

Thunder rumbled in the far distance. She hugged herself in search of warmth and looked up in time to see a flash of white lightning down by the river. She threw her head back and let the raindrops wash her upturned face. "Great God," she cried out. "Where am I? What can I do to be safe? . . . Oh God in Heaven, hear me, hear me!"

She paused and waited while the rain poured harder, the thunder drew closer, and the lightning splintered the sky above her head. The water had now soaked her clothes clear through to her skin. She shivered and trembled. Even so, she felt safer out here with the rain than back at the castle with Anna's ravings and Onkel Jan's Bible readings. If only she could cuddle up in a warm dry place with the Oma she remembered from so long ago. If only!

Maria clutched her ruby stone and wept hard and long under the linden tree.

4

ARE YOU GOING TO DIE, OMA?

APRIL 1567

"Maria, my child. What are you doing out here in this driving rain, on my pondering bench?"

Maria was so lost in her thoughts and sadness, she hardly recalled where she was. She heard the voice coming through the rumble of thunder and incessant pouring of rain. Startled, she opened her eyes and looked up into a kind and familiar face framed by a white headdress.

"Oma!" Instinctively, forgetting for the moment to be afraid, she reached out to her grandmother, and the older woman gathered her in her arms. Layers of soggy cloth squished between them for a long moment. Maria wanted to hold her forever.

"We must get you back to your room and into some dry clothes before you catch a cold," Oma said.

Maria and her grandmother began the long trek through the garden and up the pathway and the road to the castle. The thunder and lightning were moving off into the distance away from the river now. But the rain continued to fall in heavy sheets. Mud filled Maria's shoes and made her slip on the pathway. A whipping wind bit at her cheeks and hands.

All the way, Oma walked close behind her. Maria felt strong arms constantly reaching out, ready to catch her if she fell. This was the Oma she remembered, a good woman who always made her feel loved, protected, safe. Not the bad woman Duchess Margaretha had prepared her for.

When they reached Maria's bedroom, Oma left her in Toske's care to help her into dry clothes. Oma shook her head and looked somber, which was difficult for her. She had a mouth that perpetually turned upward into a pleasant smile, and her eyebrows rose in hopeful little arches above compassionate eyes.

"When she is dry, put her to bed," Oma said to Maria's maid. Then, to Maria she added, "Too much rain on a chilly spring day can make you very sick. I am going to prepare for you a hot broth and potions to protect you from nasty humors of the throat and chest."

"Whatever is a humor?" the girl asked.

"Humors?" Oma paused. "They are those strange substances in your body that cause illness. Strange and mysterious. We know very little about them, but that they can make us ill, or even cause our deaths, we have no doubt."

"Oh!" Maria responded, feeling as if she knew no more than before she'd asked.

When Oma had moved swiftly out the door, Toske asked, "Where did you go, Your Highness? I worried so about you."

"Did Oma worry too?" Maria asked, between sniffles. "And Father?"

"Once we knew that you were gone, we all worried. Thank God the countess found you—not injured, but only soaked through to the skin."

Maria smiled and gave Toske a little hug.

Toske slipped a nightdress over Maria's head and asked, "You're not going to tell me what happened?"

Maria shrugged. What could she say? That she had run away from the demons in Onkel Jan's Bible? That she feared Oma was dying? She said nothing more—and neither did Toske—until Maria climbed into bed. The bed was as big as the one she'd had at court, but its curtains and spreads were plain, not brocade. The walls were mostly bare, with only a small crucifix or painting here and there. Maria lay, her entire body still shivering, with the covers tucked in around her chin, a pile of pillows propping up her head, and a pair of warming bricks at her feet.

"Turn on your side, child," Toske said, "so I can dry your hair with this towel."

While Toske vigorously rubbed her hair—because she simply had to know and didn't want to ask Oma—Maria blurted out: "What kind of a Bible does Onkel Jan read from?"

"What kind of a Bible? I don't know much about such things. Why?"

"Remember what the duchess told me about the Protestant Bible and demons and Anna's madness? You heard her."

Maria rubbed her arms with her hands in desperate search of warmth.

Toske went on drying her hair with the towel. After a long silence, she stopped, moved to where she could look Maria straight in the eyes and spoke with gentle motherliness. "As I said, I don't know much about these things, but I can assure you of one thing. The demons Duchess Margaretha warned you about do not live in this place."

Maria didn't understand. "But why, then, did she tell me there would be heretics here who would deceive me into believing they were nice people? What was she talking about?" The memory of her words made her shudder. The duchess could be cold, but she had been kind to Maria. Surely she would not lie to her. What could she make of this?

Toske went back to her hair drying. "One thing you need to learn, Your Highness. I don't understand why this happens, but I have seen it enough times to know it is true. In the minds of many important people that live in sumptuous courts—kings and princesses and such like—strange ideas often move about. They seem to imagine that those who do not see things as they do are filled with demons."

More confused than ever, Maria closed her eyes and her mouth and concentrated on trying to get warm. Little by little, the shivering lessened. Then as she began to slip into a light sleep, she was startled awake by the opening of her door and the sound of Oma's voice.

"How is my Maaike?"

Maria had not been called by this special name since Oma visited her in Breda. She loved it. Oma always said it with a sparkle in her eye.

"Here, I have brought you something that can warm and restore you to good health." With Toske's help she spread out an array of cups, bottles, and spoons on the table beside the bed.

Maria watched each move they made. What was in each little container? Were these the magical potions Oma was so famous for? Would they be bitter?

"Now," Oma ordered, pouring a dark sticky-looking liquid into a spoon, "swallow this elixir. I made it myself."

"What's in it?" Maria asked.

"Never you mind. Just know that it will cleanse your body of all the humors that the rain has induced."

"Please tell me, Oma, I do so want to know. Since I was a little child, I've dreamed of one day becoming an herbal healer, just like you."

"Then, you have come to the right place," Oma said, lifting her spoon to Maria's open mouth. "This elixir is made of comfrey, mallow seed, licorice, and coltsfoot root," she said, "and mixed with honey and sugar to make it taste better."

Maria swallowed it, trying hard not to grimace, but barely able to get the awful tasting substance down. This was followed by a chest rub with a strong smelling paste. Oh, how it burned! Finally Oma gave her a hot spicy drink that felt ever so soothing as it went down.

"This will warm you clear to your toes, " Oma said.

Maria sipped and smiled up at her grandmother. "Thank you, Oma. Now I grow warm again. I am sorry that I made extra work for you. I never thought when I ran away . . . I just . . ." How could she explain to Oma any more than she could to Toske about all the strange and fearful questions that had sent her running out into the rain?

"Has something made you afraid?" Oma was sitting on the edge of the wide bed, looking at her with concern, her eyes smiling.

Maria ran her finger around the rim of the big cup in her hand and looked at the little puff of steam rising from the liquid. "Maybe."

"You find it frightening to move away from those you love?" Oma asked. "Even when you know you are also going to be with other people you love?" Then pausing for a moment, and nodding, she added, "I know how that feels."

How could Oma know what she was thinking? Maria looked up, searching for something in Oma's warm eyes. "You know how I feel?"

"Oh yes, it happened to me, too."

"When you were young, Oma?"

"I was eleven years old, the same as you, Maaike," Oma said, smiling quietly.

"Really? What happened, Oma?"

"It was this way. My father was a nobleman, Count of Stolberg and Wernigerode—two cities."

"So, did you move from one of these to the other when you were eleven?" Maria asked.

"No, not quite so simple. We always moved about from one place to the other—the whole family went together. Every year, we spent some months in Stolberg, then we went to Wernigerode for some months, and then back again. I was accustomed to traveling about. However, when I was eleven years old, I actually moved away from my parents to live with my uncle and aunt in another city far away."

"Why, Oma? Oh, how sad! I didn't want to leave my father when I went to Brussels two years ago, either. I have missed him very much."

Oma put her hand on Maria's forehead and offered her a smile that felt like a hug.

"I know exactly what you mean. Of course, I moved to a good place—to live with my aunt and uncle—Count Eberhard and Countess Katarina von Konigstein. You see, they had no children and my parents had fourteen. So it was decided that my older brother, Lodewijk, and my younger sister, Maria, and I would live with them."

"Oh," Maria sighed.

"I loved my aunt and uncle," Oma went on, "and wanted to help make them happy. They gave me all that I needed to have a good life in their home. They treated us as if we were their children. In fact, when my uncle died, Lodewijk became the Count of Konigstein in his place."

"So, you were happy there? And did you ever see your parents again?"

"We saw them occasionally. It was a long ride, but we did it one or two times every year. And at feast times, they would always send us gifts. My aunt was a wonderful mother to me. She trained me well in all the household and healing arts so that I could become the wife of a nobleman one day."

"What kind of things did she teach you?" Maria's body was feeling warmer, and Oma's story fascinated her. As old as she was, Oma seemed to remember what it was like to be eleven years old—and afraid. And she wanted to talk about it.

"My aunt taught me how to supervise all that happens in a castle—the butchering, the baking, the growing of the gardens. And I learned to entertain the guests that stopped by our castle for a night while on a journey or for a long family visit. I especially loved learning to grow the herbs, to harvest and prepare them, to give them to the sick people."

"Will you teach me about the herbs, Oma?" Maria interrupted. "I so much want to know all the secrets those little plants hold. I felt them beckoning to me down in the garden today."

Oma smiled, her face crinkling, her eyes sparkling until she looked almost like an eleven-year-old herself. "Oh yes, my child," she said, "I've just been waiting to teach you all I know. Someday you may become the great healer lady of the Dillenburg. Would you like that?"

"Oh my, so very much I would like that, Oma!" Maria felt the enthusiasm building to the bursting point.

"You will also attend my school, here at the castle," Oma went on, "for the children of noblemen from far and near. There every child learns many skills to prepare them for a useful life. Most important of all is the reading and writing—especially useful, since the coming of the printed book, and the German Bible."

"Did your aunt and uncle teach you these things too?"

"Yes, they did. I especially loved writing letters. I wrote to my family. And to this day, I still write to them. They are now spread over the different parts of Germany and a few live yet in the Low Countries. It is terribly important to write letters to encourage those we love, to trust in God, to be of good cheer, and to live upright lives in this difficult world."

Oma continued, her hand on Maria's shoulder, "The most important thing, my dear Maaike, is to trust in God to give you courage to handle every day. I know it may be difficult learning to live in this new place. Things are not the same as they are in the court at Brussels. Our furnishings do not sparkle as brightly. We are not kings or duchesses here, just simple noble people. This is but a country castle."

Maria shifted uneasily in her bed. "Oh, Oma, I like it here." She looked away. "Well, except for Anna's outbreaks." Then turning back, she said, "I truly like the quiet and living with plain furnishings, and the friendly servants. It's just that . . ."

"It's just what?" Oma asked. Maria felt the woman's gaze on her downcast head. "Tell me what is troubling you, child."

How could she tell her grandmother that she feared the demons Duchess Margaretha had warned her about? No, she must be careful. One thing, though, she could ask. If only she had an answer to this, perhaps the rest of her fears would go away—in time. Still not looking up, Maria twisted her night-dress with nervous fingers beneath the blankets and stammered, "It's . . . it's you, Oma."

"It is I? What about me causes you to fear, child?"

Maria sat quietly for a long moment. She clutched at the ruby necklace hanging at her neck and forced out the words that simply had to be spoken: "A—are you going to die?"

"Oh! Yes, someday I shall die. Everyone dies someday."

Maria looked up at her cautiously. "I mean now—soon!"

"Now? Soon? My no, child, not that I know anything about!"

"Then you are not deathly ill?" She looked straight at her, searching her eyes for the slightest flicker of uncertainty. All she saw was surprise and something that made her feel safe again.

"No, no, no! Where did you get that idea?"

"Duchess Margaretha told me that we were coming to see you because you were ill and wanted to see me one more time before you died." Her heart beat very fast as she told her deep and painful secret.

"Ah! So that is it!" Oma sighed. "Yes, it all comes clear now."

"It does? Why did she lie to me?"

Oma sat thinking for a long moment. Then she moved closer to Maria and, taking her by the shoulders, spoke gently, "I must begin by telling you something difficult. Your father is a most important man in this world, Maaike."

"He is?"

"Yes, he is a leader of a cause that is both just and dangerous. He has many enemies who may wish to hurt him—and his family."

"Father has enemies? Why do they want to hurt him?" Could that be the reason why the duchess sometimes says awful things about him? Was she his enemy too?

"It is difficult to explain," Oma said carefully, each word spoken as if it were a fragile piece of glass she feared breaking. "Let me say this. Many people of the Low Countries have begun to read the Bible and have learned new ways to worship God. But King Philip wants to force all people to do things his way and kill those who refuse. Your father knows it is never right to kill anyone for what he believes—or for reading the Bible. He is committed to helping these people gain their freedom. King Philip's men are determined to remove your father from their pathway."

Maria gulped and tried to understand what she was hearing. "But what has all this to do with Duchess Margaretha's telling me that you were dying?"

Oma closed her eyes, sat back in her place, then opened them again. Slowly, she answered, "My child, if your father was in danger, so were you. Perhaps your father told the duchess that I was ill and calling for you so that she would let you come to me."

"Oh, but she is not my enemy! She would not hurt me, Oma, I know she would not!" Maria threw back her heavy covers and pounded the bed in front of her.

"No, she is not your enemy, Maaike. Nor would she hurt you."

"Is she father's enemy then?" Maria demanded.

"No, I think she is not your father's enemy either."

"Then why does she talk so unkindly about him?"

"I don't know all there is to know about this. But I have heard it said that Margaretha of Parma is herself anxious to leave Brussels. Her brother asks her to enact rules she sometimes thinks are cruel. Another regent is on his way even now, from Spain, to take her place. The Duke of Alva is his name, and being a man, he will lead the king's armies and wage war on your father and his friends. He is the enemy of all who would be free to worship God as they please. He would do much harm to you and to your father."

"Does the duchess know that?"

"I am sure she does."

"Then why would she not protect me?"

"That's exactly what she did when she let you go with your father."

Maria sat stunned, staring at her hands, now lying in her lap before her. "Oh, Oma," she cried out, "how very, very sad!"

Maria reached up, and Oma took her in her arms. Burying her face in Oma's shoulder, Maria whispered, "I'm so glad you're not going to die."

"And tomorrow your herbal lessons shall begin," Oma said, smiling.

Maria looked into the warm, inviting eyes of her grand-mother and decided that even if Oma was a heretic, just maybe she had nothing more to fear. In time, she would know, but for now she felt perfectly safe.

5

THE HOUSE OF MIRACLES

MAY 1567

The month of May at the Dillenburg promised a fair and balmy summer to come. Warm sunshine filled the castle grounds on one of these glorious mornings. In its warmth Maria hurried from the dining hall, just at the end of the breakfast Bible readings, and scurried across the courtyard and around the corners of three buildings. She came to a stop in a pool of golden light outside a plain wooden door, tried the handle, and found it locked.

She moved toward a window set just high enough that she had to stand on her tiptoes to see inside. Pulling herself as high as her body would reach, she peeked through the cloudy glass panes and gazed into the little room. This was Oma's apotheek, the place where she collected her herbs, then mixed and brewed them into aromatic medicines that cured the people of the castle on the hill and the village down below of their painful, chilling, and deadly ills.

Every day since she'd moved here, Maria had come to peek into this secret room. Her thoughts and dreams about this place and the glimpses she had stolen through the window filled her with a magical kind of anticipation. No other place so excited her imagination.

Finally, today, Oma had promised to take her into its hallowed sanctuary and to introduce her to its wonders. Maria could not wait. She gripped the little metal windowsill with her slender fingers and strained every muscle to see what lay on the other side.

Tables, shelves, books, an open hearth in one corner, clumps of something plantlike hanging from the rafters—all blurred together through the wavy glass. Every day as she looked, she tried to make out the outlines of the treasures just beyond her reach. And with each frustrated visit, her curiosity had grown until today she thought she could not contain herself one more minute. She must go in and see without the glass veil, and smell and touch and taste! How long would Oma take to get here? Tingling with impatience, her fingers itched to open the door on a new world of delicious prospects.

So intently was she watching and dreaming that she never heard Oma's skirts swishing across the cobblestones toward her. Just suddenly, she was there unlocking the door and speaking her cheery greeting, "You are ready for your lessons, I see."

Maria sprang back from the window and faced her grandmother.

"Oh, Oma, oh yes!" she nearly shouted.

Maria clasped her hands together in an attempt to keep her eyes and voice and the rest of her body from betraying how excited she was. It seemed as if the sun would rise and set while she waited for the key to be turned in that old lock and the door to open and let her in.

At last the door creaked open, and she floated across the threshold into the room of her dreams. The sights she'd seen through misty windows were now perfectly clear. And there was so much more! Standing outside peering in, she had not seen half of the wonders this room contained. On all four walls, rows and rows and rows of shelves and drawers and bins reached from floor to rafters. She saw boxes and bottles and jars and baskets of every size and description and could only imagine what the drawers and bins must hold out of sight. From the rafters hung huge bunches of herbs—some dried, some still drying. They rustled in the breeze when the door swooshed open.

"Oh, Oma!" she cried in delight. "This is more wonderful than my wildest dreams. And the smells!" She breathed in deeply. "How strong, how sweet, how . . . Oh, I can't find words for it."

Oma smiled as she closed the door, then moved to a table on the far wall, just below a second row of leaded panes. "Shall I introduce you to my treasures, one at a time?"

"Oh yes, yes! Please!" Maria stood in the middle of the room now, hands still clasped, and twirled about, trying to take in all the wonders in a single turn. The swirl of her skirt just above the floor made her feel elegant. The strong fragrances made her almost giddy.

"Come, Maaike," Oma said, beckoning her to the table where a pair of large books lay. "Let us begin here."

Maria floated across the room to her side. She looked at the big books with their bulky dark brown leather covers. One of them lay open, and Oma pointed to its thick, unevenly cut pages.

"This book is called an herbal," she said. "My daughter, Juliana, and I have worked for many years to bring together all of these recipes for cures. The paper for these pages was made by my servants out in the shed behind the castle."

Maria reached tentatively toward it. Oma nodded. "Yes, you may touch it."

Maria ran her fingers over the rough texture of the paper. She noticed the intricate lines penned in heavy ink and the wonderful drawing of an herb. Somehow, she felt as if she were touching the plant itself and taking the words into her soul.

"This page is one I especially wanted you to see."

"It is beautiful, Oma. Who drew the picture?"

"Ah, it was an artist who lived here for a time with us. But that is not the thing most special about the page."

"What then?"

Oma pointed with her finger, at a scrawl of letters at the bottom of the page. "Can you read the name penned here?"

Maria squinted at it, moving her head nearer, then farther away. She examined each difficult letter, searching for a clue. "Anne von . . ." she began. "I don't think I can read the rest of it." Surely it was not Anna von Saxony, her mad stepmother.

"Anne von Egmont. Does the name mean anything to you?"

"Ah, that was my mother's name!" Maria gasped, then held her breath.

"Yes, child," Oma said, moving her own hand across the page, almost reverently. "This was the work of your mother's hand."

Maria shook her head slowly and looked at the page with new eyes. "My mother wrote this? In her own hand? What is it?"

"It is her recipe for the curing of dangerous green wounds."

Maria's heart felt as if it had stopped beating. She ran her hand over the page again, this time as if hoping something of her mother's life might remain in the ink and come to her through it. Without looking up, she added, "She was an herbal healer, too, like you, Oma?"

"Well, not quite. She did have her own little garden and she had recipes her mother had given to her. She learned to mix and prepare some on her own as well. You know, every noblewoman must know something about the herbal arts. It is expected that we will at least know how to care for the physical needs of our families and households."

"Did my mother live here at the Dillenburg with you?"

"No, but I visited in the castle at Breda once or twice while she was still living. We talked about the herbs, because she loved them too. She showed me her garden and let me use several of her recipes."

Maria looked on quietly for a long hard moment. At last, with her finger still resting on the page, she heard herself saying, "I wish I had known my mother."

The room fell silent. Then Oma laid a wrinkled hand on hers and said, "I think she left a part of herself in the words she wrote on these pages. Now, when we read them together and follow her recipes and make some of these cures, you will at least know a little bit about what she was thinking and what she loved." She paused, but Maria didn't speak. "Actually," she added, "I need to make this recipe today, for a patient down in the village. You will help me, won't you?"

Maria looked up into her grandmother's eyes and smiled. "Oh, yes, Oma."

"Now, we begin by reading the instructions. Would you like to say your mother's words aloud, while I listen? Then we can assemble the ingredients and go to work."

Maria gripped the book with both hands. She felt a little thrill of excitement run through her entire body. Never had she held such a special book. Surely Oma already knew every word she was about to read. Yet she was going to listen to her read them.

Maria adjusted the position of the book until it was just right, with the scant light from the window filtering through onto the page. *"A Cure for Greene Wounds,"* she read. *"Also useful for softening hard swellings, and swellings in the joints, for consuming cold tumors, blastings and windie outgrowings."* She stopped and wrinkled her nose at the page. "Whatever are blastings, cold tumors, windie outgrowings?" she asked.

Oma laughed. "Just a lot of big words to you, eh?"

"Very big words!" Maria paused. "But what do they mean? Did my mother know all of this?"

"I'm sure she did. But it's nothing that we are concerned with just now, Maaike. Every cure is good for something. Many are good for more than one purpose. If I told you all of it now, you would not remember the half till time for the evening meal. Just read the recipe."

"But which of those illnesses does your patient have that we can cure with this medicine? Is it one that I can understand?"

"Yes, Maaike. My patient tripped over a log and fell while searching for wild mushrooms in the woods. She has a severe wound on her arm. I was not called to look at it until already it was green and hot."

"Green and hot? That sounds very bad. Is it?" Maria wanted to learn all about what made people sick, and how they could be made well.

"Oh yes, hot, green wounds are putrefying—like rotting meat—and can lead to death."

"Ah, I thought so." Maria felt a special pride inside, as if she knew some things all on her own.

Oma went on, "I have given this woman several pots of your mother's recipe. Almost her wound is healed, but not quite. A few more pots and she should be finally out of danger."

Oma patted her apron with her hands and said, "Well, now go on with the recipe."

Begin with the roots of Marsh Mallowes, the leaves of common Mallowes, and the leaves of Violets. Boil them in water untill they be very soft. Drain away the little water that is left. Stamp the leaves in a stone mortar, adding thereto a certain quantitie of Fenugreeke and Linseed in pouder; the root of the Blacke Bryonie and some good quantities of Barlowes grease. Stamp it all together to the form of a poultis and apply very warm to the wound.

"So now, shall we go to work?" Oma was already bustling through the little room, in search of the ingredients Maria had read about.

"Show me where we might find all these things," Maria begged. "The mallows and violets need to be boiled."

"Already done," Oma announced. She went to a shelf and retrieved a low, squat jar filled with dark, limp leaves. They looked like spinach greens that had been cooked far too long to be appetizing. "I boiled these yesterday, knowing we must have them in readiness for this morning's lesson."

Oma pulled a round stone bowl from the back of the working table. "This is called a mortar," she said. Then holding up a short, stick-like piece of stone with a rounded point that fit into the curve of the bowl, she added, "And this is the pestle. Here, Maaike, you put the cooked leaves in the mortar and smash them into a fine mushy substance with the pestle."

Maria held the cold stone tool in her hand and watched as the leaves and roots yielded to the work of the stone and turned, just as Oma had said, into a fine mush. "Ach, but it's slimy," she said, scrunching up her nose and feeling the way she did when her brother had once made her touch a frog.

Oma laughed. "We will change that!" Then she sent Maria to the shelves to gather up the rest of the ingredients and let her add them one by one to the leafy mush. Her fingers trembling slightly with the excitement, Maria mixed well with each addition, watching the texture change. The powders made it pasty, the Blacke Bryonie gave it a slightly grainy feel. When at last she mixed in the grease, it turned into a beautifully smooth salve.

Finally, with great delight, she scooped up a fingerful of the new medicine and said with a triumphant smile, "Oh Oma, what a beautiful salve! And we made it ourselves!"

"You made it, Maaike!"

"With my mother's recipe!" The sound of her own words echoed in her ears like a soft, clear bell.

Oma was patting her apron with her hands, looking at the mixing table as if getting ready to clear away the mess, and saying, "What a good first lesson! This afternoon, after the meal, we take our salve to my patient in the village."

"*We* take it?" Maria questioned, her finger still laden with the result of her morning's labor. "You mean you will let me go with you?"

"But of course, you will go with me," Oma said as they began to fill the jar that once had held the soggy leaves with the newly formed salve. "It's all a part of the same job."

When they'd finished cleaning and putting everything away and were headed out the door, Oma said, "After the noon meal, we meet here again to pick up my apothecary case and go on our way."

Maria lingered in the doorway, looking back. She wanted always to remember this place as it was at this moment. Yes, she would be back again, of course. Hadn't Oma said this was only her first lesson? But would it ever look quite the same again as it did now? She shuffled her feet in the rushes, then inhaled deeply, as if to take in all the delicious fragrances and carry them away with her.

When they'd both stepped out into the balmy morning air, Oma held up a small twig of a dried herb. "This is lavender," she said.

"Is that what I saw hanging in bunches from the rafters?" Maria asked.

"One of many things you saw there. But I want you to keep this one."

"For me?" Maria felt something turn somersaults inside her chest.

Oma smiled. "A reminder of your first herbal lesson. It speaks to you of devotion and virtue—two things you will always need if you are to become a true noblewoman. It will

cheer you on a gray day, with its purple color, and its aroma
will add beauty to the room where you sleep."

"Thank you, Oma!" She sighed, almost forgetting fearful words about heretics and demons and Protestant Bibles.
Surely, she would always be safe here after all!

6

THE HEALER LADY— AND HER BOOK

MAY 1567

The day kept its promises—and so did Oma. By afternoon, when she and Maria descended from the castle to the little village that huddled at the foot of the hill, the sun had turned the world into a resplendent fairyland. Trees in fresh new greenery were waving and curtsying in the light warm breezes. In the dips and creases of the roadway, a few puddles lingered from yesterday's blustery showers. The sparkling diamond shapes twinkling on their surfaces and the lacy patterns of dried moisture around their edges gave evidence that summer was on its way.

They stopped at the garden halfway down the hill. Oma snipped sprigs of borage and put them in the basket Maria carried.

"A good healer always takes freshly snipped borage to her patients," Oma had said.

"Because it makes them glad?" Maria asked. Everybody knew that borage was good for lifting the spirits and making people happy. All her life, the girl had nibbled on the tasty leaves and knew from experience how powerful they were against unhappy humors of the soul.

"Because it makes them glad, indeed," Oma said, her words bouncing to the rhythm of her steps on the packed dirt of the road. "And because gladness is often the final medicine to make the difference between the life and death of a patient, anything that brings gladness must be a part of every cure, no matter what the ailment may be."

"Now that the weather is warm," Maria ventured, "maybe not so many folks will have ailments to be cured as in the harsher months of winter and spring." The sun felt so inviting and soothing that the girl could not imagine ever being sick with phlegm and a heavy chest again.

Oma chuckled. "One can always hope," she said. "In truth, the summer brings more than its share of showers—and phlegm. And even when there are no showers, it seems the heat grows oppressive and the stinging insects plague us. More children fall from trees and break their bones. Sometimes even the sun causes illness when it grows too hot and too bright. Always there is work for the herbal healer lady."

Oma's voice seemed to overflow with compassion. Was every healing lady so kind and gentle? Maria looked at her grandmother trudging by her side. A special kind of warm coziness seemed to reach out to her from this wonderful woman with the mouth that always smiled and the heart that always loved. Being with her grew more and more each day like being at home—safe, and comfortable. Was this the way she might have felt with her mother, if she'd had a chance to know her?

Maria had never felt quite this way before, with any of the women who cared for her. Not even with her dear sweet Toske who'd been her nursemaid and companion since as far back as she could remember. Certainly not with Duchess Margaretha, who taught her many wise things, yet withheld the thing she most craved—warm affection.

The memory of the duchess from Brussels made Maria shudder. From someplace far in the back corner of her mind, she heard Margaretha's voice warning her, "In the Dillenburg, there are demons and heretics. Beware! Let no one get too close—not even your closest family member."

Maria's heart cried out in strong resistance. Next to her father and Philips Willem, she felt closest to Oma. And Oma was no heretic! She had her questions about Onkel Jan. He was the one who always read from that big Bible. Maria still worried about it. If the Bible had been the thing that turned her stepmother mad, how safe could she be listening to it? Not that she could do anything about it. She tried always to close her ears. Maybe that would help.

But it was Onkel Jan who read from the Bible—not Oma. Yes, it looked as if she listened quietly when it was read. But maybe she wasn't really listening either. And if she was, maybe listening wasn't so bad if you didn't read it for yourself. Anyway, no matter what she might question about Onkel Jan, she had learned that it was safe to love Oma—and to let Oma love her in return.

She sidled a little closer to Oma and purposefully set her steps in perfect rhythm with Oma's. Yes, she could be trusted. It had to be so.

They were passing, now, through the cobbled streets, past rows of attractive buildings—shops on the ground floor and homes above. They had shiny glass windows, bright red rooftops, and half-timbers embedded in their walls. Children scampered everywhere, playing with knucklebones and balls and hoops and calling to one another in excited happy voices. At every step, people stopped what they were doing to look at Oma, and smile with a curtsey or bow and a pleasant greeting. *They must love her a lot,* Maria decided.

When they'd reached the end of the main street where all the shops bordered the strip of cobblestones, Oma led her around a corner and to a stairway that took them up behind the butcher's shop. At the top of the long stairs, they knocked and were greeted by a woman in an apron. Her face was as round as her body. But her eyes looked tired, and her mouth didn't smile.

No wonder Oma brought borage, Maria thought.

She invited them into her tiny, dark kitchen with its open pit fireplace and assortment of gray pewter plates and mugs lined up along a high shelf above the table. A strong odor of butchered meat, smoke, and rancid grease filled Maria's nostrils and made her stomach churn.

She noted a dingy rag wrapped around the woman's left forearm. A little girl of probably four or five peered out from behind her mother's skirt with sober, saucer-like eyes.

"Have you taken good care of your mother?" Oma asked the girl, a cheerful note in her voice.

The girl didn't answer, but hid her face. Oma chuckled. "Come, Hilda," she said to the woman. "Sit down and let me take a look at your wound. I have brought my granddaughter, Maria, today. She is my new helper."

"You going to be an herbal healer someday?" the woman asked, still not smiling.

"I should like that very much," Maria said.

"Your oma is the best healer around for teaching about powerful cures."

By this time they were all seated on a long bench at the simple table in the middle of the room. Oma was examining the wound from one side, and the little girl was peering at it from the other. "See?" Oma said. "It's so much better!"

How ugly it looks, Maria thought. *And Oma says it is better? At least it's not green. Not even a bright red.* Maria swallowed hard. If this was better, how awful it must have been before.

"Maria helped me to prepare this fresh batch of salve," Oma was saying. "It came from her mother's recipe."

"Her mother was a healer too?" the patient seemed startled. "Then, she'll do real good. I got to say this recipe's been working miracles for me!"

"Indeed it has," Oma said. She spread a fresh coating of it on a clean cloth and put it over the wound.

Hilda patted her new bandage. "It feels always so much better when you put on a clean rag. I try so hard to keep 'em clean, but there's so much to do, and it seems like everything is just plain dirty in a butcher's house. You going to read to us, Highness?"

Read what? Maria wondered. The recipe didn't say anything about reading. Oma hadn't brought the herbal book along. Surely she didn't need to read the recipe for it to work.

"As soon as I've put all these things away, I will read to you," Oma said, packing strips of cloth and a small wooden salve paddle into the big black bag she'd carried from the castle. "I'll leave the little jar for you. Now, you put on a clean cloth with fresh salve every day till I come back. Who knows how like a baby's flesh it may be next time we see you?"

When Oma had packed the last item into her bag, Maria watched her reach down inside a pocket on the outside of the bag. She pulled out a large leather book with gold on the edges of the pages.

Maria stared. *Ah! She really brought the herbal! But no, this is something else!* She stifled a gasp, holding her breath and cocking her head to one side then the other, trying to make out the words on the cover. Then, Oma turned it upright, and it lay flat on the table. Now there was no mistaking anything. The words were as plain as the eyes on Oma's face: HOLY BIBLE.

No! It could not be! Oma reading a Bible to her patient? Maria felt suddenly frozen clear to the core of her bones.

The next terrorized moments tumbled past like a bad dream. She watched Oma leafing through the big Bible until she seemed to find the place she wanted to read. All the while, the butcher's wife was calling in her children from the far corners of the house, settling them around the table, shutting little mouths, and turning her eyes toward Oma.

How they adore this woman—and her book! Maria didn't know what to do. Should she yell at them all to run for their lives from this dangerous book? Snatch the book away before it was too late? Speak up in front of everyone in the room and ask Oma for an explanation?

No, she couldn't do any of those things. She could only sit and pretend all was well—just the way she did in the dining hall five times every day. At least, she did not need to listen. She'd close her ears, busy her mind with other matters—maybe puzzling over what other fine recipes she might find from her mother's pen in Oma's book.

But once Oma's soft voice began reading, Maria forgot all about pens and recipe books. Like some irresistible fascination, the words that Oma read captivated her, made her listen:

The heavens are telling of the glory of God
and their expanse is declaring the work of His hands.

Maria felt a catch in her throat. The words were beautiful! Oma looked up from her book and into the young eyes focused on her from around the table. "Have you ever stood gazing on the beautiful blue sky with its white fluffy clouds?" she asked.

Heads were nodding and faces shining all around the circle.

"Do you know what they were saying to you?"

Every head moved slowly from side to side and each face wore a puzzled expression.

"These verses tell us what they are saying. They are shouting loudly and clearly that our God is a great and powerful God," Oma explained. "Next, this lovely Psalm of David's says that 'Day unto day pours forth speech, and night to night reveals knowledge . . .' The passage of the days and nights is telling us the very same thing."

Suddenly Maria realized she was caught up in the scene before her. Oma was reading about the sun coming out of its chamber in the skies to shout to the world that God is our maker. It all sounded so good, so safe. What was there here to make anyone mad?

Then the picture from the Book changed. No longer was it about the beautiful world God had made. Now, it was all about how good the Bible was!

"The law of the Lord [that is this Bible] is perfect, restoring the soul; the testimony of the Lord [also the Bible] is sure, making wise the simple."

No, no, no, Maria told herself, *I must not listen any more.*

Oma went on and on for what seemed like forever. Maria kept looking out the window to see if the sun had set yet. She twisted her hands in her lap and tried ever so hard to sit still. Words flew past her, and she sent them on their way, but here and there a word used to describe the Bible lodged in her mind, and she could not shake it:

"Clean . . . wise . . . true . . . sweet . . . more desirable than gold."

Whatever did it all mean? One thing seemed sure—Oma obviously thought the Bible was a good thing. Surely she knew what was right. And she was not mad. But how could it be? Duchess Margaretha was also a wise woman—cold, but no less wise. And she thought this same Bible was dangerous.

Who was right? Maria's confused mind felt like a battleground for angry clouds, lightning, and thunder.

At long last, she heard the word she knew would bring this painful reading to an end. "Amen."

She watched Oma put the book back into her bag. How gently she handled it! Yes, no doubt about it, Oma loved this book as much as Onkel Jan did.

Maria shivered. *What does this mean? What can I believe? Whom can I trust?*

7

CAN THIS BOOK MAKE ME MAD?

MAY 1567

Maria said her polite "good-byes" like a proper noble lady and hurried down the stairs and out into the warm afternoon with Oma, not getting so close this time. A few billowy clouds hovered between them and the sun. Her legs felt almost wobbly as they made their way over the smooth cobblestones in the street, then along the rocky pathway toward the castle.

Everything inside her was screaming out the big questions: *What is the truth? Is the book cursed or not? And if she couldn't trust Oma, whom would she ever be able to trust?* But whenever she opened her mouth to ask Oma about it, something held her tongue.

Her feelings ran in odd channels. Oma no longer felt cozy and warm and motherly and safe to her heart. And yet she did, too. Whenever things grew so confusing, Maria missed Philips Willem more and more. He could explain it to her.

"Are you well, my child?" Oma asked.

"Very well, thank you," Maria all but whispered. She felt as if she were watching a dream from the sidelines, looking on in fear. She could not bring herself to say another thing until they had reached the pathway to the herb garden. Here, she stopped and found words to ask, "Oma, may we stop for a moment in the garden?" Something about the garden felt secure, sheltered as it was from prying ears.

"Do you need something there?"

"I need to ask you a question."

"Then let us sit on the pondering bench," Oma offered. Smiling, she added, "Questioning and thinking is what it is for, you know."

Soon, they sat side by side on the old stone bench. Fragrant herbal shrubs brushed against their feet in the walkway and a cool, dampish wind tugged with increasing strength at their skirts and aprons. They both sat in silence for a long moment. Oma waited, looking straight ahead. Finally she said simply, "What is it that troubles you, my Maaike?"

Maria clasped and unclasped her hands in her lap. She opened and closed her mouth several times. Finally, looking at the clump of silvery-green burdock nudging her toes, she barely spoke above the voice of the wind.

"You made me frightened today."

"Frightened?" Oma said. "How did I do that? Did you find it unpleasant to have to look at the healing wound?"

"No, not that. It was ugly, yes, but I shall grow accustomed to such sights."

"What then?"

Maria could not resist the gentle warmth in her grand-mother's voice. Taking a large swallow and hugging herself with both arms, she said, "I've never heard you read from the Bible before, Oma . . . I thought . . . only Onkel Jan ever did that."

"Why did that make you afraid? It is God's book, child. Had you never heard it read before you came here?"

Maria shook her head and glanced sideways at her grandmother. The mouth with the perpetual smile kept on smiling. The eyes with all that love kept on smiling too. "No, never," she said.

Oma sat up straighter and rocked her whole body forward and backward on the bench. She put her black bag on the ground and folded her hands in her lap. "Aha, I see! And why did my reading of the Bible frighten you, then, Maaike? What is it you're afraid of?"

"The Bible, Oma. That's what I'm afraid of."

"Where did you learn to fear the Bible, my child?"

"Oh," she began, then paused and bit her lip before going on. "It was at the court in Brussels."

"Hmm! What dreadful tales did you learn there?" Something in Oma's matter-of-fact tone made Maria want to tell her more.

"I learned that the reason my stepmother is mad is that she grew up reading and learning about the Bible—the Protestant Bible. That is what you were reading from today, is it not?"

"Yes, it is, child. The same Bible you've been listening to every day, ten times a day, in the dining hall. Has it never frightened you before?"

"Oh, yes, Oma, it always frightens me. In fact, that was why I ran away to this place that first day you found me here. Since then, I take care to stop my ears when Onkel Jan reads it. Until today, I thought maybe you did the same—that only Onkel Jan read from the book."

Maria stared into Oma's eyes and saw gentleness. "My dear Maaike," Oma said, "you have been greatly misled."

"Oh, Oma," Maria blurted out, "I am so fearful of becoming mad—like Anna!" She clasped her hands now extra tightly. She must be brave.

Maria felt Oma's hand touch hers. At first she pulled back. But Oma's voice once more calmed her. "Oh my, we need to think about this carefully. You have nothing to fear, you know—nothing at all!"

"How can you be so sure of that?"

"Look around you at the Dillenburg. Every single one of us listens to the Bible every day we live. Most of us have listened to it for many, many years. We have read that Bible in this castle since the day your grandfather and I came here to live. Now tell me, Maaike, how many mad people have you seen walking the halls of the Dillenburg?"

"How many? You mean besides my stepmother?" Maria's tongue turned to jelly in her mouth.

"Yes, who else? Are any of the servants mad?"

"I don't know, Oma."

"Have you ever seen one of the cooks or the horse groomers act mad, like Anna?"

"N-no," she stammered.

"How about my other children—Tante Juliana or Magdalena or any of the others?"

Maria lowered her head and shook it slowly.

"Your father? Have you seen him mad?"

"Oh, no!"

"Your Onkel Jan? He who reads from this book ten times a day within your hearing. Have you ever once seen him play the madman?"

"No, not even Onkel Jan." Maria felt a sense of wonder creep into her heart.

"Is it I, then, who seems to be mad?"

Maria could scarcely contain the confusion any longer. "No, no, no! Oh, Oma, I have seen nothing to make me think anyone here was mad. But . . . but . . ."

"But what?" Oma held her hand snugly and looked deep into her eyes, waiting for an answer.

"But . . . the wise Duchess Margaretha in Brussels told me that if I read the Protestant Bible, I too, would go mad. Why would she—" She couldn't bear to finish the thought and trembled inside until her whole body seemed to shake.

Oma folded Maria into her arms and said softly, "It is difficult, Maaike, but we must learn that no one knows everything—not even the wise Margaretha von Parma."

"But how could she be mistaken about such an important thing, Oma?"

"Ah, 'tis sad but true that many people are taught ugly things about the Bible. And they may have never read so much as one tiny verse from the holy pages. It's quite likely that Margaretha's mother and father and those who trained her planted in her a superstitious fear of the Bible. She probably thinks that, except when the religious leaders are studying it, the Book breeds snakes and demons."

"Yes, I heard her say those very words one time. Are you saying it is not true then?"

"Have you seen snakes and demons during our Bible reading time? Ever? You saw how eagerly my patient and her children flocked to me to hear the reading today. They have learned wonderful things from the Bible, Maaike." She raised her eyebrows and added, "And they all seem to me to be free of Anna's malady."

Grandmother and granddaughter sat quietly among the trees and fragrant herbs for a time. Maria felt the trembling in her body begin to relax in the warmth of Oma's closeness. At length, she asked, "Oma, tell me, did your mother read to you from the Bible when you were a child?"

Oma chuckled. "Ah yes, did she? Not quite. You see, it was this way. Back in those years, we had no Bible to read in the language that we spoke. All Bibles then were written only in Latin, read only by priests and professors of religion."

"So when did you first see one?"

"I was already engaged to be married before I saw one. But, all the years I was growing up, I had teachers who read to me little bits and pieces of it. Both in my home in Stolberg, when I still lived with my parents, and later with my tante and onkel. You see, there was a man named Martin Luther who was translating the Bible into German so we could read it. While he was doing this, he was also writing many fine sermons and printing them. My teachers obtained his pamphlets and passed on their contents to us in our lessons. They had many Bible verses in them."

"So, you didn't fear that snakes and demons would spring at you from the Bible?"

"No, no, we learned to read the Bible as God's book written especially for us. We were taught to love it, to respect it, to ask always what God wanted to say to us from it."

"My father, then. Did you read it to him when he was young?"

"Ah yes, like all my children he grew up hearing it every day."

"Just like Anna!"

"Well, maybe I did not teach it in the same way as Anna's parents. That I cannot say. But Willem learned as much Bible growing up as Anna did, that I can tell you. Even from the beginning, it was as it is now in the school that the children at the Dillenburg attend. Bible lessons are required of all students. Why, even you have had some of those lessons, have you not?"

"I . . . uh . . . I have tried not to pay attention in those classes, Oma. I was afraid." Maria stared at her feet.

Straightening herself beside the girl, Oma spoke like a school mistress, "But now you have no more need to tremble, eh, so?"

Maria felt a faint smile playing with her mouth. "It really is not true, then, what the duchess told me?"

"No, Maaike, it is not true, at all."

"Then, you say I should have no more reason to fear?"

"No, my child, none at all. Now, I think I hear the dinner bell ringing. We must not be late."

Maria stood to her feet and walked right next to Oma all the way to the evening meal. For the first time since she'd come to the Dillenburg, Maria sat at a meal in an almost fear-free silence, waiting, until she heard the voice of Onkel Jan bursting out: "The heavens are telling of the glory of God."

She looked over at Oma whose smile gathered her into her heart. Yes, it was going to be all right after all. She knew it now.

8

A Messenger in the Night

14 February 1568

Many months passed on the Dillenburg hill. The whole place bustled with the daily activities of aunts and uncles and cousins and a host of servants too many to count. Delivery wagons and messengers on horseback added to the mix, along with dogs and ponies and important visitors of many sorts—and children learning their lessons.

With each passing day, Maria grew more comfortable with her new home and the school for noblemen's children under Oma's supervision. Here she learned to read fine literature and play fine music as well as to sew and spin and cook and manage a household. Most of all, she learned the social graces of the nobility, along with principles of godly character and how to worship God in the little church on the side of the hill. Each day, it seemed, she came to fear the reading of the Bible less and less.

Spring bloomed into a glorious warm summer. Maria and her classmates spent many carefree days with Oma and her daughters, Maria's aunts, harvesting herbs and wild flowers that grew in profusion in the garden and along the roadsides. Fall followed and brought its own crop of flowers to cut and hang from the rafters of the apotheek. Then the snow began to fall and turned the old castle hill into a magical fairyland.

In the middle of all this, though, something happened that began to gnaw at Maria's insides—just a little in the beginning, but growing worse and worse. In November, when Anna birthed a baby boy named Maurits, what should have been a happy occasion turned into a terrible nightmare.

Maria could never forget that awful night Maurits was born. Anna had howled and carried on without ceasing for hours and hours. When Oma went to deliver the baby, Anna sent her from the room and ordered her servants to lock the door.

"I will not have this cursed woman touching my baby!" she screamed. Then she shrieked and wailed loud enough for the whole castle to hear. She demanded that her personal servants go find her a midwife from a neighboring village.

Maria couldn't understand it. Oma was the best midwife anywhere. Every baby in Dillenburg and many others for miles around had been brought into the world with her skilled hands. When, after the birthing, Oma sent herbs to help restore the new mother to health, Anna poured them out at her husband's feet and cursed at him as well. Why did Anna hate both Oma and Father so much?

Baby Maurits turned out to be weak, scrawny, and sickly, like two other babies Anna had borne. Those two had died within months of their birth, and no one expected Maurits to live out a year.

From that day forward, Maria felt a dark cloud of sadness hanging over the castle, and it brought with it a long string of unhappy events that seemed would never end. The winter that began as a fairyland display felt longer and bleaker than any winter Maria had ever known.

To everyone's surprise, Maurits survived day after day. But his life did not bring pleasure to anyone. He cried a lot, and so did Anna. Early in the New Year, the family took the baby down to the little stone church for a service of baptism. Maria watched in fascination as the family gathered round the baptismal font and the pastor of the church sprinkled water on his little head. In the light of a hundred candles, he prayed over the boy, and dedicated him to "a life of holiness and service to Almighty God." All the while, Anna frowned and made unpleasant noises. Father Willem ignored her strange ways and looked on at the proceedings with what appeared to be great pride and joy.

For the next week or more, up at the castle, the Dillenburg came more alive than ever with a huge feast to celebrate the baptism. Family and friends and acquaintances of Father Willem, Anna, and Oma came from far and near. As with the birthing, it should have been a happy time.

But thanks to Anna, nothing was happy. From the beginning, she yelled ugly words at Father in front of the whole company of guests. All through the week, she sat in dark corners pouting, or she drank too much and staggered around acting totally deranged. She treated Father as if he were to blame for all her unhappiness. She scowled or sneered at him, and scolded him whenever he chanced to come close. Maria shivered at each new outburst of the woman's anger.

In the middle of one dark, moonless night in mid-February, Maria came suddenly awake at the sound of the hunting hounds echoing over the hilltop. This was not an unusual sound at the Dillenburg. The dogs howled all day, every day, as residents, messengers, and visitors moved in and out of the gates. But nighttime was another matter, and rarely was the starlit peace of the old castle disturbed. Maria knew immediately that whatever had caused this terrible commotion, it must be a fearsome urgency.

"Another messenger?" she said, bolting upright in her bed.

Before she could pry her eyes wide open, she heard the scuffling of feet outside her door, moving down the passageway toward her father's apartment. In no time, there came a banging on his door followed by a flurry of excited voices.

"Who's waking Father before daybreak?" Maria pulled the covers up around her shoulders and felt the pounding of her heart. "No, no, not more bad news!"

Ever since Anna had birthed Maurits, it seemed that the arrival of messengers bearing tragic words had grown nearly constant. Had this woman's mad actions and evil words placed a curse on their whole world? Maria didn't know much about curses, but she believed they existed and that one could seldom find a way to be free from their power.

Maria was rarely told the content of the messages that came these days, but sooner or later she would hear about them. Servants seemed to know—or to think they knew—what was going on. And the stories they gossiped to each other in her hearing often struck new terror to her heart. With time, she usually managed to learn the truth, but even that was usually not good news.

In December she'd learned that the Duke of Alva, the new governor who had come to replace Duchess Margaretha, was a cruel man. He frightened many people until they fled from the Low Countries just to be free from him.

In the beginning of the New Year, it was said, he rounded up eighty-four prominent citizens in the old city of Brussels, where Maria had lived for two years. He called them heretics—that word the duchess had used. On a series of giant scaffolds in the public square, he hanged them all, putting fear into the hearts of every person who did not want to be ruled by King Philip of Spain.

A couple of weeks later, this same duke summoned Father Willem and Onkel Ludwig to appear before him in his court which was called the "Blood Council"—whatever that meant. It gave her a chill just to hear the words. The duke claimed that Father and Ludwig were guilty of high treason.

What was high treason? Maria wondered. And did the Duke of Alva intend to hang Father like the others?

If Father and his brother didn't come by the date the duke ordered them to come, he threatened to take away all of his possessions in the Low Countries—his castles in Breda and Brussels, his fine silver and tapestries.

Ah! So that must be why Father had removed his prize belongings from Breda. Where he'd hidden them she never knew, except for a few things she recognized in their apartments here in the Dillenburg. All she knew for sure was that Father and Onkel Ludwig had no intention of appearing anywhere near where the duke could get hold of them. She'd heard Father himself say that.

The whole castle was abuzz with talk about a war that her uncles were planning in the Low Countries. Onkel Adolf had come home from some far country to join them. Of course, war was a way of life in Maria's day. Being a soldier was a part of protecting one's lands and families, as a nobleman. Maria watched the young boys in Oma's school practicing their marching, swordsmanship, and target shooting out in the fields around the castle.

It was no secret, then, that all the men in the family had been trained to be soldiers and had fought in a variety of wars. Maria's father was actually in France fighting at the time when her mother died. Toske told her about it once long ago.

And ever since they'd come to the Dillenburg, Father seemed always to be holding secret meetings in the old knights' hall, behind the huge wooden doors. Just what it was about, she didn't understand very well. She only remembered what Oma had told her about the Duke of Alva bringing an army to kill all the people who refused to do things the way King Philip insisted. It sounded ominous to her.

And now this messenger in the night. What could it be?

Maria fingered the ruby her brother had given her. She reached to her bedside table for Oma's twig of lavender, put it to her nostrils, and breathed of its fragrance. All the while, she listened to the strange voices and scuffling feet in the night. The servant seemed to move away, and the hunting hounds greeted him as he passed out of the castle gate.

It all happened in a flurry! But the rest of the night passed slowly. Maria only dozed now and then, constantly holding her ruby and wishing with all her heart for Philips Willem to appear in front of her. If only Maria could know that Anna had not actually brought a curse down upon them, she might find reasons to hope these awful events would soon end.

If only . . . But she could not change the way things were.

The next morning Maria made her way through old, dirty snow to Oma's apotheek. She loved nothing better, even on such a bitter cold morning, than to work here with Oma and the herbs. Over the months since she'd come to the Dillenburg, she'd learned what lay stored in most of the bins and drawers and bottles and what hung from the rafters of this wonderful world. She now knew many of the recipes in the old books by heart.

Yet there was always more to learn. She couldn't wait from day to day to see something new—to smell some new fragrance, feel some new combination of textures, discover some new healing property of one of the herbs. Oma's apotheek was the one place where clouds of worry evaporated with rays of hope and excitement. Indeed, every time she stepped across the worn threshold and let the big door close her in, away from the rest of the world, this place seemed to hold her as much in its spell as it had that first day last spring.

This morning, though, she sensed a cloud even here. She and Oma set about their work with little to say. Maria knew her task for the day—grinding dried herbs to a powder, mixing a fresh batch of poultice for rheumy chests that so often plagued them all on these nasty winter days. But her mind weighed heavy with thoughts of last night and the hunting hounds.

At breakfast, her father had looked so sad! More sad than she'd ever seen him. She longed to climb up into his lap, as she did when she was little. If only she could coax him to tell her what was wrong! But she knew if she were to question him about last night, he'd simply pat her on the head and tell her it was nothing for her to worry about. Young girls didn't need to know what was going on around them. Or so she'd been told all her life. Usually, this was good enough for her—but not this time.

How she wished for enough courage to ask Oma about it. She knew what the answer would be there too. "Let your father do the worrying." She'd heard it many times before. But just this once, she determined to find a way to get a new answer.

For a long while she ground away at a bunch of dried goldenrod flowers. Again and again she rolled the pestle over them until they were crumbled, then pulverized. Yet she kept grinding—each stroke with greater energy.

Suddenly she heard her own voice begin to speak. "Oma, do we have an herbal recipe that could cure my father of his sadness?" It startled her.

Oma looked up from the pot she was stirring over the fire in the corner, her mouth round and her eyes resembling a pair of question marks.

Maria went on. "He seems so very sad all the time, and this morning, I thought his heart was broken completely in two. Oh, Oma, what can we do to make him feel better?"

Oma went back to her stirring and Maria continued grinding the same bunch of goldenrod that had long ago been turned into the finest powder a mortar and pestle could produce. The air between them felt as if a thundercloud were about to explode and send out lightning.

"Oma," she tried again, "I . . . I know Father had messengers in the middle of the night. They wakened me. They came and went so quickly, I was certain something dreadful had happened. Please tell me, is Father in great danger? The duke who threatened to take away his castles, will he come here and take him away too?"

Oma stopped her stirring once more and half turned toward her. "Oh my dear child, Maaike," she said at last. "The world is in such a turmoil, and . . ."

"I . . . I know young girls need not know what goes on, but Oma, it is so hard when I see my father looking always as if he will break into a hundred pieces. We are healers, Oma. Surely there is something we can do!"

There, she had said it: the thing her heart had held as a secret for so many months. She stood staring into the mortar, her eyes not seeing the goldenrod powder or the recipe on the table beside it or her fingers that trembled. Her breath turned to steam and curled around her nose in the cold room. And she waited.

After some time, Oma lifted the big metal spoon from the kettle on the stove and hung it from the hook above the fire. Slowly she walked to Maria. Standing straight and tall, as Oma always did, she laid a hand on the girl's arm, looked into her eyes, and said softly, "No, Maaike, the Duke of Alva will never come here to take your father away. He has no power or authority over us in this safe place. That is why you are here."

"But, something is wrong, Oma. I feel it in my heart. Please tell me what it is!"

In the silence that followed, a new thought came to Maria and struck her like a thunderbolt. "Is it Philips Willem?" She grasped her grandmother with strong fingers. "What has the duke done to my brother?"

"No one has harmed him," Oma reassured her hastily.

"Then what have they done to him that puts him in danger?"

Oma simply looked at her for a long moment. Maria saw a flicker of confusion in the deep gray eyes. *Was Oma afraid too?*

At length, Oma straightened, patted her apron, and put on a happy face that seemed not at all to be real. "The duke only threatened to kidnap him and take him away," she said too easily. "But the messenger has gone to bring him here immediately. All will be well, you will see. He should be with us in a few short days now."

"A few short days?" Maria felt the words seep out of her like a long, weakened sigh. No, she knew they would be long—the longest days she had ever known.

"Maaike, we must wait with courage and trust in our God who loves both us and Philips Willem—loves us far more than we can know."

"How can we trust that, Oma?"

"His book says, 'Cast your care upon Him, for He cares for you.' I've seen it happen, child—a thousand times at least. I know it pains us deeply, and the wait can feel impossibly long, but He will take care. And we have each other to hold us up."

Maria stared at her grandmother for a long, uneasy moment. She sighed, then shook her head and said wistfully, "I hope you are right, Oma."

She dumped the goldenrod powder into a bowl and began to grind once more. Neither she nor Oma spoke again all morning, and when the dinner bell sounded, they went out together to the dining hall.

A fresh snow was falling, covering up the dingy ground and transforming the landscape into a fairyland once more. Maria felt her heart strangely lifting with the falling of each new feathery flake on her nose.

"He cares for you!" rang in her ears. *Oh God, please let it be true! And could you care for Philips Willem, too?*

9

A Few Short Days?

28 February 1568

Oma Juliana's "few short days" grew ever so slowly into two long and dreary weeks. Maria went to bed each night with a heavy heart. Would she ever see her brother again? She fingered the ruby necklace that never left her neck and seemed to grow heavier each day as the weight of missing him grew. She slept fitfully and awoke each morning with less hope than she'd had the night before.

She tried hard to greet each day with hope as she dropped quickly from her bed to the floor, wrapped her robe close about her, and looked to the window high above her bed. Staring up at the flurrying snowflakes, and, holding tight to the small ruby stone, she would repeat, over and over, "Maybe today. Surely he has spent the night in some nobleman's house just around the bend on the Dill River. Yes, today is the day."

Every day it was the same. But in her heart, Maria knew it was an empty habit. Philips Willem never came.

On the last day of the month, everything changed. She came awake to the sounds of a gentle knocking and the familiar voice of Oma. "Maaike, are you awake? I have news!"

Startled, half frozen with fear, she stumbled from her bed and went for the door. She unlatched it and let Oma in, along with an enormous blast of frosty air.

Oma gripped her by both arms and looked her straight in the eyes.

"At last, we have news of Philips Willem," she said directly.

Maria trembled. "Only news? Then he has not yet come?" She searched Oma's eyes for a flicker of hope and found only deep concern.

"He *is* safe . . ." the pause at the end of Oma's short words felt ominous.

"B . . . but where is he?" Maria felt panic rising in her.

"In Spain . . ." Oma bit her lip and went on, "with King Philip."

"But why? He's not coming here, then?" Maria waited for her grandmother to say something, but Oma remained silent. She could only guess what that meant. "I'll not see him again, will I?" Maria turned her back to Oma and returned to her bed where she sat staring at the rushes covering the floor.

"Just as I feared, all along," she moaned.

Maria's whole world had turned to ice in these few seconds.

Oma moved haltingly toward her, speaking in disjointed phrases as she came. "The Duke of Alva . . . he kidnapped him . . ." She paused, then finished lamely, "before your father's servants arrived there to bring him home."

"Why?" Maria heard her own voice explode and fought to hold her body still.

Oma was sitting beside her on the bed now. She also stared at the floor. "To make your father sad, Maaike," she said simply. "These men—the duke and the king—they are your father's enemies. Oh, my—" Oma broke off. Then mumbling as if to herself, she said, "How grateful I am to our God that you are here with me."

"But, Oma," Maria pleaded, "Philips Willem was my only close friend. I have no others like him—friends, brothers, sisters—none. All the cousins here are younger than I—and most of the students in the school as well. How shall I live without him, especially knowing he is in the hands of Father's enemies?" She wrung her hands and fought back tears.

"I know it is difficult for you," Oma said, her voice weak and lifeless. "All you can do is to learn to trust in God to take care of us all—and that includes Philips Willem."

Maria felt as if a huge storm were brewing inside her. "How can I trust Him when He does not bring my brother home to me?"

Oma didn't answer. Instead, she placed her hand gently on Maria's. Maria felt her presence like a warming fire. Something about this special woman could make her feel cozy and safe when all the rest of the world around her was cold and cruel.

"Trusting God is never easy," Oma said at last.

"For you it is," Maria said, her words quick and short.

Maria's grandmother shook her head slowly, and a sad little half-smile spread over her face. "No, Maaike, that is not so. To trust is always hard. I, too, must struggle with it. Always. Always."

"You struggle? No! You're always so calm and happy."

"You only see what I let you see, child. I have memories and pains and doubts you know nothing of."

"You mean there are times when you can't trust God, either?"

Oma nodded. "Let me tell you a story, Maaike, so you will understand that what I have told you about trusting God is indeed true. It happened when your father was eleven years old, the same age as you were when you came here to stay." She paused. "The same age I was when I went to live with my aunt and uncle."

Maria tried to imagine her father, a child eleven years old, walking through these corridors and sleeping in a room like hers. "What happened?" she asked. "Did the king kidnap him, too, the way he did Philips Willem?"

"No, not exactly," Oma nodded slowly as her thoughts traveled back in time.

"It was like this. Your father had a wealthy cousin, Rene, Prince of Oranje. He was a friend of the king, Emperor Charles V, father of King Philip of Spain. While Rene was a soldier in the Emperor's army, he was killed during a battle in France. As he had no wife or children to inherit his lands and titles, his will left everything to his nearest cousin. That was our Willem." She stopped talking and folded her hands in her lap, appearing thoughtful.

"Lands and titles?" Maria asked. What was this all about?

"It meant, Maaike, that at eleven years old, your father now had houses and lands and a whole long string of lordly titles to go with them. He was—and still is—Prince of Oranje, Count of Nassau, Catzenellenboghen, Dietz, Grimbergh, Arlay, Nozeroy, Lord of Chatelbellin, Lieutenant General of the Netherlands, Governor of Brabant, Holland, Zeeland, Utrecht, and Friese, and Admiral . . ." She paused and took in a deep breath. "It nearly takes my breath away just saying all those long titles. And I think there are more that I can't remember."

"Oh my!" Maria's mind was spinning, trying to imagine the immense importance of all that Oma had said.

Oma sighed. "I shall never forget that day when the messenger brought the news. At first, we were pleased and proud that our son would now be wealthy and powerful far beyond anything we could have given him."

"Was Father glad too?" Maria asked.

"I think he hardly understood what it meant, at first. Nor did we. But soon enough, the messenger told us the sad news that went with the good."

"What was that?"

"It turned out that if Willem was to inherit all those lands and titles he would have to go to Brussels to claim them, and he would have to stay there, perhaps forever."

"Oh, no!" Maria gasped.

"Yes," Oma said. "He lived in the very same royal court where you lived before you came here."

Maria looked at her grandmother, scarcely believing what she'd just heard. "But why couldn't he wait until he was grown up to go away?" she asked.

"Oh, Maaike," Oma said, then stopped and said nothing for a while. "You see, it was the Emperor's plan to take him away from us so he could train him to be a prince of the kind he wanted him to be. He insisted we must either send Willem to live with him—or someone else would be chosen to receive the inheritance in his place."

"Ach, Oma, how dreadful! And they wouldn't let you go with him to court?"

Shaking her head solemnly, and brushing at a tear on her cheek, Oma answered, "Oh, no! The emperor would not permit that either! His sister lived in the court too, and he appointed her to be both a mother and a teacher to my son." She spread her hands and shrugged. "So you see, they really did not need me." Sadness filled her voice.

Maria gasped. "Oh, Oma, how awful! You must have missed my father so dreadfully! Like the way I miss Philips Willem!"

"Oh . . . I did . . . I did!" Maria heard the hesitation in each word as if they were swords piercing the woman's tender heart.

Oma sighed. "At the same time, I had a house full of children to care for—four from my first marriage, one of my husband's by his first marriage, and seven younger brothers and sisters of Willem's. And in the next years, God gave me four more. They kept me busy. But each child is precious. It was very difficult, and all the more so because for many years we never had a letter from our absent son. Except when one of my husband's servants traveled there and brought us word, we heard nothing."

"So, is that when you found it hard to trust God?" Maria suddenly knew that she and Oma shared a grief much greater than she'd realized.

"Hmm," Oma mused. "If I am to tell you what went on in the depths of my being, I will say, yes, there were days when I was afraid to trust Him. Like the day we put Willem on a fine horse that had been sent to us from the emperor. I'd made sure all his prize possessions were packed in the wagons that went with him, even though I suspected his new 'mother' would find none of them acceptable and would throw them all away.

"I stood beside him in the courtyard and made myself smile when I told him good-bye. He looked so young and small going off on that big horse into a world too large for us to imagine."

Maria's eyes filled at her own memories of the day she herself had watched Philips Willem set off for Louvain. She remembered the tears, the anguish of spirit, the fear she felt that day.

"Were you afraid, Oma?" she asked.

"Very much afraid," she answered. "I remember standing in the courtyard and watching till his caravan had gone down the hill and so far along the road beside the Dill River that I could no longer see him. Then I ran back into the castle and went to the chapel and got down on my knees and wept and wept. I even remember the prayer I prayed that day."

"You do?" Maria tried to imagine her grandmother on her knees weeping inconsolably. Somehow it did not fit the strong and cheerful woman she knew.

"I said these very words, 'Oh God, You know I tried to find a way to keep my son here. But his father insisted, and I had to let him go. Will You go with him for me and protect him as he goes? And, please, help me learn to trust You with my son.'

"I remember the words, because I went back there and prayed them over and over again, day after day, until they were burned into my soul."

"Did you finally learn to trust Him, Oma?" Maria asked.

Oma shrugged her shoulders and nodded slowly. She smoothed Maria's hand with her own. "It took a long time before I could truly believe. But eventually I learned that God could be trusted."

"When did you *know* it?"

"I think it was the day Willem first came home for a visit. I saw all his fine, rich clothes and wondered if the boy I'd sent away was still in this young man's body. When he came closer, I looked in his eyes and I knew. I've since wondered many things about my son, but never again could I doubt that God had answered my prayers." She paused, then folded her hands in her lap and added, "Now, once more I must trust, as all of my sons go off to war in these coming days. It will be difficult, but . . ." Her voice trailed off into silence.

Neither of them spoke for a long, long while. Maria thought about her father and brother and about the king and the duke and their horrible schemes. At last she asked, "Oma, what if those ugly people in Spain teach Philips Willem to hate our father? Do you think he could become Father's enemy, too?" She felt a shudder run through her body.

Oma rocked backward and forward on the bed and looked thoughtful. Then she placed her finger under Maria's chin. She looked so deeply into her eyes that the girl felt it far down in her soul. "My dear, dear Maaike, two things: First, I cannot believe all the kings and dukes on earth could ever turn Philips Willem's heart to hate his father. But more, this day you begin to learn life's biggest secret."

"I do?"

"Yes, you do. It's simple to say and often hard to do—and remember, no one knows that better than I."

"What is it?" Maria asked.

"The secret lies in these four little words: Trust God with everything!"

Maria didn't answer. It didn't sound simple to her.

Oma went on, still looking deep into her eyes, "It may be a long time before you will see your brother again. But you can trust God to keep him safe and not to let him learn bad thoughts and ways in that difficult place."

"I don't know, Oma. I'm so afraid for Philips Willem." Maria shook her head slowly and avoided her grandmother's gaze.

"You will see," said Oma. "Just give yourself lots of time. At any rate, no matter what may happen, if you worry and fret, it will do no good either for you or for your brother—it can only make you a sad young lady. That must not be!"

Again the room remained totally silent for a long, long time. In Maria's mind, pictures of Father Willem and the king and the duke and her beloved Philips Willem were clashing about. Would she ever be able to sort it out and know what was right?

At last Oma said in a tone more like her cheerful self, "Ach! It's nearly time for the bell to ring calling us to breakfast. You are still in your nightdress. We will talk later." She stood, brushed her many skirts into place, then patted the side of Maria's face once gently and passed quickly outside into the cold.

Immediately, Toske hobbled into the room. How she seemed to limp these days!

"Good morning, Maria," the graying old woman said with her customary smile. "Not much time this morning to prepare for breakfast."

"Yes, Toske, I know it," Maria responded absently.

Most mornings, as the beloved servant lady helped her wash her face and put on the many layers of her dress and braid and pile her hair atop her head, they talked idly of things that did not matter. But this morning, scarcely a pair of words passed between them. As soon as possible, Maria dismissed her, then sat on the edge of her bed waiting till the breakfast bell had rung and the sound of feet heading for the dining hall had ceased outside her window.

When she was certain no one was about, she donned her warmest cloak and fled down the snow-covered hill in search of Oma's pondering bench. No one had walked the path to the garden in weeks, and Maria had to tromp through snow halfway up her leg. She set each step down with a decided crunch and a desperate prayer. "How can I trust you, God?"

At the entrance to the garden, she surveyed this spot she always considered such a sanctuary from trouble and pain of soul. A blanket of crusty snow had turned everything, from the tiniest bushes to the hedge fence, into indefinable lumps and blobs of whiteness. Icicles coated the bare branches of the trees and hung in ghostly shapes that reached nearly to the ground.

She breathed in the crisp morning air until she felt it sharp in her chest. Then, looking up at an amazing blue, blue sky, she spread her arms wide and cried out, "Does anybody out there care that I just lost my best friend in all the world?"

The gate was nearly buried with snowdrifts and frozen in place. With great effort, Maria spread her skirts over the top of it, then hoisted her body up and over and rolled and tumbled onto the other side in a deep bed of snow. Once she'd found the huge flat, bank of snow that she knew was the pondering bench, she set to work with mittened hands, carving out a seat.

Then she sat, hugged herself, and rocked back and forth in an effort to keep warm. Staring at the leafless trees, all sparkling in their iciness, she could almost believe that they were alive. She flung questions at them in the loneliness of her silent world.

"Where is Spain, anyway? And how could King Philip steal my brother away, just because he hates my father so? Does he take good care of him? Or has he put him in some damp dungeon where he feeds him only dry crusts of bread and tin cups of dirty water? Will he grow sick there and die?"

Tears were streaming down her cheeks now, in rivulets of frostiness, misted by her breath. She brushed at the tears with her mittens, but the wetness would not go away.

Would she ever see her brother again?

"Trust God with everything," Oma had said.

She'd also said it two weeks ago, when the messenger told them Philips Willem was coming to the Dillenburg. Maria had tried her best to trust God to bring her brother to her. Then today her hopes were trampled like the crusty snow with its icy crystals, ground beneath her boots. God had let that horrid Duke of Alva take her brother away. So why should she trust Him now?

Never had she felt more alone staring at the icicles glistening in the sun. But as she watched, something moved in the tree. Along the length of first one icicle and then another, she saw little streams of water sliding, sending diamonds of reflection out into the crystalline air. One by one, they dripped to the snow below. A quiet voice she'd never heard before seemed to speak inside, a breath of warmth and hope.

"The winter may be long," came the words as clearly as if Oma stood there whispering in her ear, "but the ice is melting. Take hope and watch for the answer to your prayers as well. In time God will melt the ice that keeps your brother imprisoned."

Almost, she dared to hope. Almost!

PART 2

Mad Anna
Tales of Madness
1568–1571

Borage:

I Borage
Bring alwaies courage.
—AN OLD LATIN VERSE

It maketh a man merrie and joyfull.
—PLINY

To exhilerate and make the mind glad . . . used everywhere for the comfort of the heart, for the driving away of sorrow, and encreating the joy of the minde. —JOHN GERARD

A good healer lady always takes freshly snipped borage to her patients, because it makes them glad. And because gladness is often the final medicine to make the difference between the life and death of a patient, anything that brings gladness must be a part of every cure, no matter what the ailment may be.
—OMA

10

A DAY FOR GRIEVING AND DISCOVERY

25 MAY 1568

On a rainy spring afternoon, the big dining hall at the Dillenburg bustled with warm bodies, steaming bowls of food, and delicious smells. Onkel Jan had read the Bible and prayed. Just as Maria was lifting a spoonful of soup to her mouth, she noticed out of the corner of her eye that Father Willem was not in his place. Strange! She'd seen him earlier this morning.

Also Onkel Jan had disappeared as soon as he'd said "Amen" to the prayer. She looked to Oma's place, and even that was empty. Oma never missed a meal unless she was away visiting one of her children, which she was not right now.

In the Dillenburg, there was a firm rule about the meals. Everyone who lived and worked in the castle was required to attend meals here five times every day. No one ever broke the rule, unless they were deathly ill or someone else was deathly ill and needed their attention. Maria had heard that it was Oma who made the rule, so if Oma broke it, something had to be wrong!

She let the spoon fall back into its bowl. What could it be? She recalled now that a messenger had arrived just as they were all gathering for the meal. What awful news did he bring, if Father and Oma and Jan were all needed to take care of it? *Ach!* Maria shuddered at the thoughts of Philips Willem in Spain and the onkels off at war.

Maria had stood near Oma that gray morning a few weeks ago as the men mounted their horses and said their brave "good-byes." She remembered how relieved she was that at least Father Willem did not go with them, but she knew he, too, would leave soon. She would never forget how Oma waved at her sons, until they disappeared out of sight at the bottom of the hill and around the bend in the Dill River. Then, she took out her big handkerchief, wiped her eyes, and muttered under her breath, "I fear they will not come back."

Now, two seats down from Maria in the castle dining hall, Mad Anna sat cold and stiff in her chair. Her daughter, four-year-old Anna, sat between her mother and Maria. Instead of eating, the little girl simply stared at her food and made sniffling noises. Her mother ignored her and continued eating her own meal in a painfully typical sullen silence.

Maria was relieved whenever Anna chose to remain silent. At least then she was not ranting and raving about something, yelling at one of the servants or at Father Willem or at her daughter—maybe at Oma or the whole world.

The meal lasted a dreadfully long time. Maria nibbled at a few bites of meat and bread, and swallowed a little of the drink in her cup. But how could she feel hungry with Father and Oma obviously off attending to trouble of some sort? And the two Annas to her left sulking at the edge of their plates? Baby Maurits was screaming from his cradle in the corner of the room. His mother would not attend to him, and the servants who did could not get him to stop his howling. If only Onkel Jan would come back and read and pray so they could leave this awful room.

Just when Maria was sure she could bear it no longer, Onkel Jan did reappear standing behind the reading desk, as if he'd never left his spot. He opened the big Bible and prepared to read while Maurits continued to cry.

"Today our hearts grieve," he began, "for we have received sad news."

Anna stirred suddenly in her chair, the first indication she'd given since the meal began that she knew anything was happening around her. She leaned forward, one elbow resting on the table, and looked at the man who read. Maria could not see her face, but she felt anger in the air and knew Anna's wild eyes held daggers. She'd seen that look before. Maria trembled.

Onkel Jan went on, apparently unaware of the storm brewing in Anna's corner, "But first, before I pass on to you the words our messenger has brought to us, let us meditate on Jesus' comforting words to his disciples as He approached His dying hours with them:

" 'Let not your heart be troubled. You believe in God, believe also in Me. In my Father's house are many dwelling places . . . I go to prepare a place for you. And if I go and prepare a place for you, I will come again, and receive you to Myself; that where I am there you may be also.'

"I conclude with the words of the great apostle Paul, 'Therefore, comfort one another with these words.'"

Anna began to howl. Maria recognized that familiar low moaning sound that came so often from Father's and Anna's apartment. It blended with Maurits's cry, which was finally growing fainter. Onkel Jan stood silently at his reading desk for a long moment. He had a somber face that always made him look as if he were on the verge of scolding the whole world. Today, though, his face looked softer and very sad. He stared at the desk, and Maria watched him struggle to speak. Maria suspected a welling up of tears in his throat that drowned his words.

At last, while Maurits whimpered and Anna moaned, Onkel Jan spoke, his words choked yet simple: "Our brothers, Ludwig and Adolf, have won an important battle against the enemy in Friesland. May God be praised." He paused and cleared his throat. "Our brother, Adolf, has fought as our brave champion, but in fierce combat with the Spanish commander, he gave up his life—a sacrifice for the cause. The Spanish commander suffered a like fate."

He paused while a volley of gasps filled the room, then turned into a soft buzzing of distressed voices. He lifted his hand and said, "Let us pray."

Maria only half heard the prayer that followed. As soon as the amen sounded, Anna shoved her chair back from the table with a great clatter. She stood to her feet and banged on the table, then brushed the dishes away with her hand. Midst the sounds of breaking and clanging dishes, she began to shriek: "Curses, curses, curses on my worthless war-loving husband! And on this wretched prison house of the Dillenburg! These long months I've been forced to abide here like some dull peasant maiden. No one has noticed or cared that I am a princess! Where is my honor?"

She stopped and surveyed the eyes, all focused on her. Onkel Jan approached and gripped her arm. "Anna, Anna, calm now. This is a time for grief, not anger."

She threw his hand back and went on, "Stop me not, you ugly demon. I've had enough. I hate you all, you traitors. And my husband?" she drew in her lips and spat forcefully on the floor. "Horrid tyrant, selfish dreamer, murderer of his own brother . . . I will not sleep with him one more night. My days in this hellish place are over. I gather my servants and board my coach and set off for a new life filled with freedom and honor."

Had Maria heard her right? Anna was going to leave? Today? Tomorrow? When? Of course, she'd threatened to leave many times before and still she stayed. But what if this time she meant it and would really go away? Maria suddenly felt almost guilty. Why did it feel so wrong to hope she would do it this time? But the woman was still ranting.

"I take all my jewels and other valuables and leave you with ghostly memories of Anna, Princess of Oranje indeed." Again she spat on the floor. "And with your consciences—if you have any."

Then, while every person in the room drew back in horror, Anna stood erect and arrogant and, in a regal strut, pushed past the long line of tables, allowing her wide skirts to shove at chairs and people, or whatever stood in her pathway to the door. Little Anna rushed to her and grabbed at her skirts, but she brushed her off and left the girl in a tearful heap on the floor.

Finally she shoved open the door, strode out, and shrieked, "I hate you all. Adieu!" No one made a move to stop the wild woman. Her laugh, loud and hollow and evil, gradually faded into the distance.

Maria, moved by an instinct she didn't know she possessed, rushed to pick up little Anna from the floor where her mother had left her. She and the small child had never played together or spent time together. Her mother always held the girl in the embrace of her own little world.

Yet somehow, it seemed so right for Maria to attend to the poor abandoned child. It felt awkward at first, but once she'd taken her in her arms, she thought maybe she could even love her. Before she knew it, Maria was letting her own tears fall quietly into her half-sister's golden hair.

For a long time, they hugged. So much grief for one day, Maria thought. She'd never before really known anyone that died. Her mother, of course, died when Maria was only two years old, so she had no memories of that or really of her. She didn't have many more memories of Onkel Adolf she could store away. She remembered only that he was handsome and that on the few occasions she had seen him, he'd always greeted her with a smile.

But she knew Father must be sad today. After all, Onkel Adolf was his brother, and she knew how she would feel if Philips Willem died. Oh, dear, what if Philips Willem did die? Must she think about that now? But Oma! Oh, poor, dear Oma! She had just lost her son!

Maria gripped little Anna even harder and stifled a rush of hot tears.

Dear God, I think Oma does not feel like trusting you right now. She knew this was going to happen. She said so before my onkels left. Now what will happen to her?

She felt the child in her arms struggling to pull free.

"I go to Mama," little Anna cried out.

Stunned, Maria released her grip, but held her still by the hand. "No . . . we'll see her later, Anna," she said.

"We go now!" the girl demanded.

"Your mother is sick, Anna. You stay with me . . . only for now."

Little Anna burst into a howling fit. She stamped her feet and pouted and pulled free from Maria's hand, demanding, "Now! We go now!"

She shoved open the heavy door and ran out into the drizzle of a spring storm mostly spent. Maria followed, not knowing what the child might do next. They arrived in the courtyard just in time to see Mad Anna's coach, the one she'd ridden in all the way from Breda. Creaking and swaying, it lumbered behind a team of fine horses driven by their coach-men toward the hill and the gates of the castle.

Little Anna ran toward the coach, screaming, "Mama! Mama, wait for Anna!"

"Anna stop!" Maria yelled, and lunged forward to stop her. Barely in time, she caught hold of the girl and pulled her to safety, but Anna was kicking and screaming and struggling against her.

"Mama! Mama! Mama!" The cries hurt Maria's ears and broke her heart.

Just when she thought she could not hold little Anna any longer, she felt a pair of strong arms embracing both of them.

A familiar voice spoke in deep tones, "Don't be afraid, my daughters, your father is here."

"Father!" Maria cried out.

Then she heard the word from little Anna too, "Father!"

How can Anna call him that? She wondered. *He's my father. She's Mad Anna's daughter.*

Father Willem was hugging both of them. Maria heard sniffling sounds coming from somewhere behind his beard. She felt the beating of his heart through his doublet. She looked up into his eyes and saw a faint sparkle there. A tear?

"Thank God I still have my daughters," he mumbled. Then he kissed each one on the forehead, and they snuggled close in his embrace.

"Maria," she heard Anna's little voice and looked over to see a small hand reaching toward her. She took it in her own and felt something new and different inside. Father was *their* father. Maria and Anna were sisters. Oh! She'd never had a sister before.

A ray of sunshine broke through the clouds and lit up the cobblestones at their feet. Maria held Anna's hand and smiled up at their father.

Sister Anna! She rolled the words around in her mind and her heart and discovered that they made her feel like part of a real family.

II

A HOWLING IN THE NIGHT

FALL 1568

In the middle of a rainy-wet night, the sound of thunder awakened Maria from a deep sleep and pleasant dreams. She could not remember what those dreams were, but she wished to go back to them. She shook her head, forced her eyes open and stared toward the high window on the far wall. A long fork of lightning split the sky and as it did, she heard a wild scream from Father's apartment.

Father Willem was away on war business. But Anna was back—and with her the noise—never-ending, wild and ugly.

"She's at it again," Maria moaned to herself. She burrowed down into her bed and pulled the covers up over her ears.

"Anna, Anna, Anna!" she continued, speaking to the underside of her coverlet. "Why did you have to return? Were you worried that we didn't have enough unhappiness here already in those months when you were gone?"

Another clap of thunder! And now the words Anna spat in a fury were much too clear and loud for Maria to miss or ignore. "I hate you, Juliana! You and your miserable son . . . cruel family. I hate you all! Do you heeeear me?" Her earsplitting cry blurred off into the sounds of drizzling rain and sent a chill through Maria.

If she hates us so much why doesn't she go away again—and stay away this time? Maria shuddered and burrowed down farther. Everything in the Dillenburg had been so peaceful and quiet for the short time she was gone. Then, two months ago, she had gone to some big celebration with Father in Heidelberg, and he'd talked her into coming home with him. The noise had not stopped since. Night after night, it went on and on and on.

Another crash of thunder followed this time by the sound of breaking glass—or was it pottery? Yes, she was drinking again, staggering around, swinging wine bottles, breaking things—probably precious things.

"Ohhhhhhh," came the loud and pitiful wail from Anna's apartment. "What a horrid, boring prison house this old castle is!"

Prison house? How deluded she was! Her brain was soaked with wine, and she was selfish and ugly in every way Maria could think. She scarcely paid her youngest child, Maurits, any attention. Now, it was rumored that she was with child again. But did she care? No! Clearly, all Anna cared about was Anna's pleasure, Anna's wine, Anna's fine clothes, Anna's wild friends.

The thunder had ceased, and all Maria heard were Anna's moaning and the splashing of raindrops on the cobblestones outside her door. Then she heard the chiming of the clock from the church halfway down the hill.

"One, two, three, four . . ." The last tones of the chime hung in a brief silence, broken by more angry shouts:

"I hate this place! I hate you all! I am going away, this time forever! Come and stop me if you will!"

For a long moment she was silent. Then Maria heard a horrendous clatter of banging noises and doors being opened. Then Anna shouted, "Servants, come quickly! We're fleeing this dreary place!"

Maria felt a flutter of excitement in her tummy. If only it could be true! If only they could be rid of this horrid woman forever. Maybe, if she went soon enough, Maria could yet get some sleep.

The noises continued, finally changing from banging and shouts into the clatter of horses' hooves and the creaking of her once-elegant coach. The hunting dogs barked to announce their passage. Maria heard Anna's demented cries until the coach carried her over the hill, out of earshot.

Slowly the dogs settled down. "She's gone!" Maria sighed. "And this time little Anna and Maurits are safe—in the care of a nursemaid."

"Thank God," she mumbled. Then she drifted off into a dozing-in-and-out kind of sleep until the roosters crowed their greeting of the dawn. Maria threw back the covers, stretched her arms into the now silent morning, and reached with her toes for the floor. A brighter day had begun!

12

A Husband to Love Me

Fall 1568

A brighter day indeed! The storm had passed, and a chill of early fall filled the sparkling air. Maria breathed deeply and hugged Meerkaatje, the Dillenburg's pet monkey, with one arm while balancing a large wicker basket over her other. She and Oma walked together briskly, and soon reached the herb garden at the foot of the hill. Around their feet scampered Hondje, a black and white mutt of a dog, with a long squarish muzzle, enormous flopping ears, and a bushy tail that seemed to wag his whole body with each excited step. Of all the dogs that lived on the castle grounds, Hondje was Oma's personal favorite, and she took him and Meerkaatje with her often on their herb-gathering adventures.

Maria loved these dewy fall mornings. The leaves on the lindens and oaks were turning red and yellow and orange, rustling softly in the breezes that blew. All the while, meadowlarks and cuckoo birds sang as heartily as if it were the middle of the summer.

There had been other mornings like this one. But today Maria felt freer, happier, and more at peace than usual. Gone were Anna's moans and screams and ugly words. For the first time in weeks, she felt free to enjoy the music of the birds, the breezes, and the barking of the hunting hounds. She looked around at her world and saw it as if for the first time.

"I love this place, Oma! It's beautiful here!" She gave the monkey an extra hug and added, "And I love Meerkaatje, too."

"Yes," Oma said, smiling. "He's lived with us here at the Dillenburg for many, many years. He belonged to my late husband, your grandfather—a gift from a friend. But of course, we all love him." She reached over and scratched him behind his little round ears.

"And now, we go to work," she said. "Let Meerkaatje roam, and you follow me as we gather the herbs needed for today's session in the apotheek."

Maria set the monkey on the ground, patted the dog's head as he brushed against her skirts, then followed Oma through the garden, carrying the huge basket. They walked up and down the rows, and Oma snipped and pruned away at the herbs. Some she discarded, others she lay in their two baskets, in neat piles. All the while she either hummed soft tunes of the kind Maria heard in church, or she told Maria what each herb was and what they would use it for. The dog and monkey scampered about, appearing now and then through the shrubbery, as if checking to make sure the humans were still there.

When Oma had finished gathering herbs for the day, she straightened up, resting her hand on her hip. She smiled and said, "Before we snip our fresh borage for the day, come, let us sit on the bench for a time."

They found their spots and Oma breathed a heavy sigh. "I'm thinking," she began, "you are happy that Anna is gone. Am I not right?"

Maria held her basket with both hands and felt shy. "Why y-yes," she admitted awkwardly.

"And it doesn't seem right to be happy when your step-mother goes away. Is that not so?"

Maria stifled a gasp and did not answer. *How does she know that?*

"I know how you feel," Oma said. "I feel it too."

"You do?" The words tumbled out before she'd had a chance to think about them.

"Yes. You know, Maaike, that Anna is married to my son. She is the mother of two of my grandchildren. I want to love her and care for her. But she makes that most difficult. Her actions grow more and more ugly each day. Because of that I find life easier when she is gone. And all the while, what I really wish is for her to act like a daughter-in-law I can love and talk with."

Oma sat rigidly as she talked. But Maria felt surely she must be trembling inside, holding her feelings in check with great difficulty. Maria struggled to follow her grandmother's example.

"Besides," Oma added, looking down at her feet, "as you know, she is with child once more." She shook her head. "She goes away to a dissipated life, carrying my unborn grandchild. I worry so for that child."

Suddenly it seemed more important than anything else in Maria's life to know the answer to the one question that had been burning in her for weeks now. Without further thought, she blurted it out. "Oma, tell me, why did Father Willem marry Anna in the first place?"

Oma sat statue-still, sucked in her breath, and held it, without looking at Maria. Meerkaatje scampered around the corner and climbed up onto her lap. She grabbed him and held him tightly. Then she let out her breath slowly and spoke in measured words. "That is a hard question, my child. You know that noblemen cannot always choose a wife to suit their pleasure. In fact, most often, their wives are chosen for them. The Emperor Charles chose your mother for Willem the first time."

"You mean the way Duchess Margaretha talked about how she would one day choose a good husband for me?" Maria asked.

"Yes, that is the idea."

"Did you choose Anna for my father?"

"No, Maaike," Oma said, shaking her head as she spoke. "I didn't choose her for him. In the end, he chose her himself. But, being a prince and a leader, it was impossible for him to choose a wife simply for love. Instead, he had to choose the daughter of a nobleman, and he felt it was important for her to be a Lutheran, to please the people of the Low Countries who were opposing the Catholic King of Spain. When he met Anna she was young and beautiful, and she fell instantly in love with him. I think he told himself it would be all right. How could he possibly know how wrong he was?"

"So he didn't know that she was mad then?"

"My no! No one knew it then."

"When did he learn it?"

Oma sighed, and the monkey leapt from her lap and chased after the dog. "It was months before your father had any idea. I think the problem was that he did not take time to get to know her before he married her."

"Oh?"

"Yes, that often happens. Most of the time, when a noble lady is engaged to be married, she is thirteen, fourteen, or fifteen. Then she marries within a few short months. Sometimes, the bride and groom do not even meet each other until the wedding—or so close to the wedding date that they do not know each other at all."

"So, Oma, is that what happened to you?" Maria looked at the old woman and tried to imagine what she'd looked like on her wedding day. It was hard to picture Oma being fifteen or sixteen years old.

"No," she said, "my story is quite different."

"How old were you, then, when you married Opa?"

"I was twenty-five when I married your grandfather," she said.

"Oh, so old?"

Oma chuckled, "Ah but you know, he was my second husband."

"He was? Who was the first one?" Maria begged.

"It was this way. My father and the uncle with whom I lived arranged for me to marry a fine and handsome young man named Philips van Hanau. He was nineteen years old on the day of my engagement. I was fourteen."

"That's only two years older than I am now, Oma." Maria couldn't imagine what it would be like to be engaged so young. She didn't even know a young man of eligible age.

"I shall never forget the occasion," Oma went on. "My father was too busy traveling in pursuit of his business to be there on that day. So my Onkel Eberhard stood with me. And Philips's parents were both dead at that time. So his guardian, a man named Willem von Nassau-Dillenburg, stood with him. Philips and I made a pledge to be married as soon as it was wise."

"Was that soon?"

"In my case, we had three long years to get to know each other. We visited each other often and became good friends. I'm not sure I knew it then, but that was a highly uncommon privilege. By the time we married, I knew Philips was the good man I would like to spend the rest of my days with. Very kind and capable, he was."

"So, tell me about your wedding journey, Oma. Did you have many attendants? Was your dress beautiful?"

"Oh my, yes," Oma said, smiling.

Maria had never seen a real wedding. She'd heard people talk about how a bride set out from her parents' home on the morning of her wedding—or days earlier if she had far to go. She rode in a coach with a number of friends who would be her wedding attendants. She wore her wedding gown and many jewels. And as they rode through the little towns along the way, people would come out from all over to throng the coach and greet the bride, soon to become their new noblewoman. They would shower her with attention and joyous shouts. Maria always wished she could see such a "Bride's Homecoming" procession, as it was called, just to get a peek at a real bride.

"It was a most glorious and exciting day." Oma continued with her story. "My dress was made of crimson red velvet and covered with gold brocade, and I wore many expensive pearls. I had so many attendants in my procession that it took eighty horses to carry them all. We rode in true glittery splendor. In the village of Bergen, we met up with Philips's procession, coming to greet us and escort us on to my new home, where the wedding would take place."

Maria tried to imagine all the gold and glitter and the magnificent horses. She listened for the creaking of the coaches, the clopping of the horses' hooves on cobblestones, the shouts of the people, the laughter of children. And to envision Oma, seventeen years old, wearing crimson red velvet with gold and pearls!

"After greeting each other, we boarded an official coach, and rode into the lavishly decorated city of Hanau followed by both his procession and mine. The city overflowed with wedding guests and at least two hundred horses. We took our vows in a ceremony, then spent several days feasting with our many guests. The kitchen of the castle that was going to be my home became a beehive of preparation—thousands of birds and fish, meat tarts and herbed vegetables served with sauces and wines. It was so exhausting that I almost rejoiced to see all the guests go home and leave me to begin to do the thing I'd been prepared by my dear aunt to do."

"What was that?" Maria asked.

"Oh, to be a loyal wife and the countess of the castle, to run the household, to care for my servants, to till and harvest the herbs, to supervise the cooking and baking and slaughtering of animals. And to give birth to and raise Philips's children."

"How many children did you have, Oma?"

"I gave birth to five of Philips's children. One of them died—Reinhard, my first—two weeks after his sister, Catharina, was born." Oma sighed. "All in all, though, those were six wonderful years."

"And then?"

"Yes, then on an Easter Sunday morning, all unexpectedly, death took Philips from us. Two days later, I gave birth to his youngest daughter. We christened her Juliana. At twenty-three years of age, I was the mother of four children, noblewoman of a large household, and brokenhearted."

"Ach! Oma! What a sad story!" Maria paused to grieve about her grandmother's tragedy before she went on. "So, did your uncle arrange for you to meet and marry my grandfather?"

"Oh, no!" Oma chuckled. "Willem von Nassau-Dillenburg was no stranger to me! He had been guardian to Philips before we married. In fact, I attended the baptism of his daughter, Magdalena. I had no idea then that one day she would be my stepdaughter."

"Then he must have been older than you, was he not?"

"Yes," Oma said, nodding. "Willem was nineteen years older than I, but a kind and thoughtful man, and he loved me very much, for all of our days together. His wife had died only a few days before my Philips. And after Philips's death, Willem came often to our home to help me to deal with the things that a young widow must handle, and to watch out for the needs of my children.

"We spent many hours in conversation of one manner or another. Further, we were both interested in the new religious ideas being preached by Martin Luther. It seemed only natural that we should marry. When he suggested it, I was more than ready to give the rest of my life to him. He was a wonderful man.

"He brought me here to the Dillenburg where I have spent all my days since. God blessed my womb and gave us twelve more children. I thank the Almighty God for two good husbands. I pray each day for my son Willem's pain in the loss of his first wife, your dear mother, and now this even more awful tragedy, to be married to such a dreadful, hurtful woman."

Maria and her grandmother sat thinking for a long while. The animals romped about their feet. Finally they stood, snipped the day's supply of borage, then gathered their herbal baskets and the monkey and headed homeward.

"Oma," Maria said as they climbed the hill to the castle, "before I left Brussels, the duchess told me that one day, after I return to the court in Brussels to live with her once more, she would pick a good husband for me."

"She told you that?" Oma asked.

"Yes. But I no longer live in Brussels."

"Nor does she," Oma reminded her. "She has been replaced by the Duke of Alva and has returned to her earlier home of Parma in Italy."

"How sad for her!" Maria paused, then added, looking at her grandmother expectantly, "So, who will choose my husband for me?"

"Your father will decide, Maaike, but I think he is too busy to think such thoughts for now."

"And when he does begin to think them, Oma, please promise me that you will not let him give me to a man who does not love and care about me the way your husbands cared for you. Please!"

Oma moved her basket from one hand to the other. With her free arm, she surrounded the girl and held her tightly all the way to the castle. "I shall do all I can, Maaike. I shall do my best. And we shall both pray to God to do for you what we cannot do ourselves."

"I would rather never marry at all than marry a man whom I cannot love and respect." Maria liked the sound of those words. Yes, she would stand by them for the rest of her life.

13

MARIA, HERE IS YOUR SISTER, EMILIE

APRIL 11, 1569

When spring came to the Dillenburg, everything exploded with new life and color. Maria loved the bright flowers blooming in the gardens around the castle. The trees covered with blossoms in white and many shades of pink looked like they had come from some fairyland dream. Most of all, she loved the way the long dark days gave way to scattered sunshine and light rain showers.

She had been here almost two years now and, at thirteen, she felt more at home than she'd ever felt anywhere. She no longer feared the daily Bible readings or looked for signs that Oma or the others might be heretics. She never supposed that demons lurked in the shadows. If only her father weren't gone so often, and to such dangerous places—and if Philips Willem would just come back—then, her happiness would be complete.

On this beautiful morning filled with sunshine, birdsongs, and blue skies, she expected all to go as usual. No surprises, no problems, no disappointments—just this good life!

In fact she was thinking about all this as she sat embroidering with the other young ladies in Oma's court school for noblemen's daughters. Here, Oma taught all her young ladies to spin and sew and then to embroider with many fine stitches and beautiful colored threads.

As she tied the last knot in a rose she had embroidered onto the bodice of a ball gown, she heard the hunting hounds barking out on the brow of the hill. With a start she pricked her finger.

Ever since last May when the hounds had announced the arrival of a messenger with news of Onkel Adolf's death, the dogs' baying made her fear more sad news. When would a messenger come with word that her father had been killed in his travels? Maria wondered. She knew he never went to the Low Countries, where the war was fought. But the war was his business, and the Duke of Alva was determined to destroy him, so how could he be safe anywhere?

Listening to the hounds howl, Maria sat tensely in her chair and waited. She threaded her needle with green floss, ready to begin stitching a leaf for the rose. But her mind was roaming outside, trying to picture the scene of a messenger arriving.

Foolish girl, she told her troubled heart, *why do you fret? It's probably just a delivery boy bringing a load of flour up from the village mill below.*

Moments later she knew that was not so. One of the household servants entered the room and moved quickly to where Oma sat by a window sewing. His face wore a dark cloud, and Maria sensed something was not as it should be. Before she could go to Oma and ask if he brought news of her father, her grandmother slipped out, following the servant into the courtyard.

Maria pretended to be sewing, but her thoughts would not focus on the flowers or their leaves. She could only wait and hope that her father was not in trouble somewhere. She felt her chest rise and fall beneath her dress. The fabric she held grew damp as anxiety caused her to perspire. Each moment she waited felt like an hour.

At last, Oma's chambermaid entered the room and scurried over to where Maria sat. "Your grandmother bids you come," she whispered into Maria's ear.

Maria rose to her feet, set aside her embroidery and fled with the woman, out the doorway and across the courtyard to the apotheek. The maid opened the door and ushered her into the herbal world that always seemed to work such wonders with her spirits. Her heart beat wildly as she swept across the threshold.

Oma sat next to the table holding a large bundle. She looked up at Maria and smiled. What was this about?

"My father. Is he alright?" Maria blurted out, not able to restrain herself but terrified to hear the answer.

Oma nodded. "We have no news of him. But what we have is an unexpected gift from Anna. Come, my child, I want you to meet someone very special and very new."

Maria held her breath and approached her grandmother with a mixture of feelings. Should she laugh or cry? Be sad or happy? She didn't know.

"A gift from Anna?" she asked, thoroughly puzzled.

Oma pulled back the covers on the bundle, and Maria saw a tiny, red face with a mat of fuzzy hair straggling over its forehead. The eyes were closed and the rosebud mouth puckered like a drawstring and made funny little twitching movements.

"Ah!" Maria could say no more for a long moment. She stared, her mouth gaping open, then finally managed, "Is it . . . ?"

"Yes, it is," Oma said. "Maria, meet your half-sister, Emilie."

Chills ran down her arms and legs. "B . . . but, what is she doing here?" she stammered.

"Anna has sent her."

"She did not come too?" Maria asked.

"No, she expects me to raise her child."

Maria could only continue to stare, her mind a blur of questions. What was this? Anna was giving away her baby? And it was Father Willem's child?

"Here," Oma said, standing to her feet, "you sit here and hold the child for a while. I must prepare an herbal bath to cleanse her when she is awake again."

Maria sat in the chair. Still dazed and without a clear thought in her mind, she held open her arms and let Oma lay the bundle there. She'd never held a fragile, new baby before.

She heard her own small awe-filled voice, exclaiming, "But she's so wrinkled . . . so red!"

"She first saw the light of day only yesterday," Oma said as she stood over her two grandchildren, rearranging the blankets and covering the infant's head.

"How could Anna do this, Oma?" Maria said at last.

Oma walked to the shelves and began pulling down bottles and jars and the mortar and pestle. "Anna is not the first mother to give away her child, you know."

"Oh?" Maria's eyes opened wide in surprise.

"Yes, remember, my mother gave away not only one, but three children at the same time."

"Ah yes, you told me about that. But you were not babies. Besides, she loved you all the same and you saw your parents often."

"You are right. They continued to visit us and send us gifts. We always knew we were their children. And they had raised us up from infancy."

Oma went on working, her fingers grinding the herbs. For a long while, the only sounds in the room were the baby's regular breathing and the gentle swishing of pestle against herbs in the mortar. Then Oma spoke again, this time in a somber tone. "Remember the time I told you about, when I had to send my son Willem away?"

"Yes, Oma, I remember well. But that was not your choice. He was taken from you."

"Indeed, I never would have chosen to let him go. And I had to pray long and hard for peace of mind to accept it."

"You worried for a long time about whether you had done the right thing for your son, didn't you, Oma?" Maria was trying to imagine how it would feel to lose a son the way Oma did. Of course, it all ended well, but Oma couldn't know that when Father left.

"I did. One thing helped me through those worrying days."

"What was that?" Little Emilie made fussy sounds, and Maria instinctively began rocking her gently.

"One day as I sat on my pondering bench, praying the prayer I told you about, I told God that He couldn't know how I felt as a mother. No sooner had I said it than I remembered that God Himself had one day sent His Son away from home."

"He did?"

Oma smiled. "Ah, yes, that was what Christmas was about, you know. God sent his Son from Heaven with all its beauties and perfect happiness, to come down here to earth and live in the midst of sorrow and pain and dirt and anger and selfishness."

"Yes, Onkel Jan has been reading about that at some of the meals."

"God didn't have to do it," Oma went on, nodding as she spoke, "but He sent Jesus because He loved us all so much. He knew that only His Son had the power to save us from our sins. So He sent Him, let Him live with many difficulties, watched Him die a horrible criminal's death that He did not deserve to die."

Oma stopped grinding herbs, folded her hands over the mortar and pestle, and looked out the windows. "As I sat there thinking about it, I knew that if God could give up His Son for the good of us all, then He could help me to be at peace about letting my son go. Maybe it was for a good cause too."

"A good cause?"

"Yes, Maria. I now know God has an important mission for your father to fulfill in the Low Countries."

"What mission is that?" Maria stared at her, puzzled.

"He must show the world what I learned from my own father and taught to all my children. In fact, it was the last thing I said to my son, when I sent him off to Brussels:

'It is never right to kill anyone simply because of what he believes.' "

"Ah yes," Maria sighed, "I've heard you say that before. Quite different from what I learned at court when I lived there."

"I can believe that. I knew when I taught it to him and reminded him of it, that it would not make life easy for him in that place. But over the years I have watched as the God who gave him this mission has taken good care of him."

Maria rocked her baby sister and pondered the whole thing for a long while, then said, "But Oma, what Anna did was not the same at all. This is her very own tiny, lovable baby. How could she choose to just give her away for no good reason?"

"We do not understand, Anna. What can make her mother's heart so shrivel that she could give up an infant, freshly sprung from her own body?" From across the room Maria thought she saw tears trickling down Oma's face and sparkling in the light of the sun shining through the window.

"Is it because Anna is a mad woman, with a melancholy too deep for borage to cure?" Maria asked, shuddering at the thought.

Oma nodded. "I think so, Maaike. And I believe sending Emilie here may be one of the wisest and kindest things Anna could do."

"What?" Maria gasped. "How can you say that?"

Oma went on working, selecting herbs, mixing them into a fine powder, as she talked. "If she kept the child with her, Anna would surely kill her with her selfish ways. At least here we have a chance to give her a good life."

"Like you are doing for Little Anna and Maurits already?"

Oma nodded.

Maria hugged the child and pondered her future. At thirteen, she knew she was old enough herself to be married to some nobleman and be the mother of a baby like this. Oma had told her that many noblewomen were married very young. In fact, had she stayed in Brussels with Duchess Margaretha, perhaps she would now be married and cuddling her own newborn child. *Ah, but someday my turn will come.*

The baby began to squirm and make high-pitched newborn cries. Maria watched a little hand appear through the folds of the blanket. She immediately gripped it in her own and held it fast.

She looked down into the little face, more wrinkled with each new outcry. "My dear little sister, Emilie," she said. "Oh how Father will love you when he holds you in his arms!"

14

ANNA RETURNS, BUT . . .

For more than two years, the Dillenburg had rest from the noise and nastiness of Mad Anna. Then, on a windy morning in March, she returned one more time.

Fifteen-year-old Maria, with her herb basket on her arm and Meerkaatje on her shoulder, was crossing the castle courtyard with Oma Juliana when the hunting hounds began to bark. She looked ahead to the road down the hill and saw a horse-drawn coach approaching.

"Are we expecting guests, Oma?" she asked.

During the four years she'd lived in Dillenburg Castle, she'd seen many unexpected things come up this road and into the castle. Messengers came on horses of all sorts. Coaches arrived with guests coming to celebrate a birthday or a baptism. When Father Willem was home, there seemed to be a stream of dignitaries coming and going to make plans for the war.

Her uncles came and went too, and she never knew when one or the other would show up—sometimes on the run from something, looking scared and exhausted. But almost never did any of them ride through the gates in triumph with a smile on his face. And rarely these days did anyone go out with the hounds to hunt hawks in the open fields, as the family had done often in the years before talk of war.

Oma Juliana stopped, gripped her cloak around her to anchor it against the winds, and gazed ahead. "I don't believe anyone is expected, child, not today, but we shall know momentarily."

Maria felt a little twinge in her heart. Whenever she watched a coach bumbling up the hillside some part of her saw and heard threatening images of Anna's face and Anna's shrieking voice and Anna's coach. It didn't seem to matter that she'd been gone for more than two years. The memories came anyway.

"Please," Maria whispered, to no one in particular, "don't let it be Anna."

Neither Maria nor Oma spoke again as they squinted into the bright light and watched the coach come closer. The only sounds were the clopping of hooves on cobblestones and the creaking of large wooden wheels, accompanied by the howling of the hounds. Then it was the hard breathing of the horses and the commands of the coachmen, as the old coach slowed to a stop before the castle door.

The coachmen stepped down quickly, and out from the wagon jumped two armed guards, large shining swords hanging from their belts. Shouting gruff orders, each man reached roughly into the coach and pulled out a scruffy prisoner with hands bound in chains. Both appeared somewhat dazed and said nothing.

One was a man Maria didn't remember ever seeing before. He hung his head and stumbled along beside his guard toward the castle. The other was a woman with unkempt hair blown about by the wind in stringy wisps. She had an enormous belly that bulged out beneath the nightdress she wore. A cape hung at an odd angle across her shoulders, giving her little protection from the cold.

Maria stared, then gasped. "It *is* Anna! In chains!"

Anna? Without her fine jewels and wide-flowing skirts and elegant headdress? Bare wrists showed beneath her sleeves, the manacles cutting into them with huge red streaks.

"I knew it would come to this," Oma muttered.

"But . . . what has she done, Oma?" Maria asked.

"The man is her lover. He's been living with her, down river, in Siegen."

Maria felt numb all over. "How do you know this?" she asked.

Oma stared at the new arrivals, then said softly, "The world is not blind, and when a peasant sees a thing, he does not long keep it to himself."

Maria sighed. Yes, she'd always known that Anna looked at other men with eyes that invited their attentions, and she'd heard the servants talk about the men they'd watched creeping along the hallways at night, toward her room. But, now she'd left Father and run off and taken a new man—in a city right under Father's nose? How very awful! Thank God that Father was not here to see this ugly sight.

Oma moved toward them, but stayed well behind and out of sight of the prisoners. Maria followed, her footsteps hesitant, feeling as if she carried a stone in each shoe. Shortly the castle door opened and Onkel Jan stood there, rigid and frowning.

One of the guards spoke to him loudly enough for Oma and Maria to hear each condemning word. "We found this treacherous man hastening to Her Highness Anna's door. And inside the house, indecently clothed, she awaited him."

"Not true," Anna shrieked. "He is my lawyer, come only to help me set my affairs in order."

Onkel Jan scowled at her and asked in a voice filled with quiet anger, "You always greet your lawyer in your nightdress and loosened hair?"

"Your soldiers here, they stripped me of my real clothes!" She spat out the words. "To make me look like a bad woman. It was planned—all planned. You sent them there yourself, oh most hateful Jan van Nassau, didn't you?" She was straining at her chains and the words came out like flames of fire.

"And you, Jan Rubens," Onkel Jan said, shaking his head sadly and addressing the other prisoner, "what have you to say for yourself?"

The man shuffled uneasily and hardly raised his head when he spoke. " 'Tis true, I am a lawyer, my lord. 'Tis also true this woman's affairs need ordering. But I cannot deny that my intention in going to her house was not to do business with her. She has seduced me with her charms and smooth words. But do know, I have done no worse than any of the other lovers she has had these past months."

"He lies! He lies!" Anna screamed.

"And what have you to say for this pregnant belly that you cannot hide, Anna?" Onkel Jan asked his brother's wife. "Has your husband been with you after all?"

Suddenly Anna grew still. She hung her head and trembled all over. The familiar moans began—then huge heartbroken sobs. Chills ran up and down Maria's back, and she grabbed Meerkaatje and hugged him for warmth. He wrapped his tail around her neck and nestled into her arms.

"Tell him the truth," Jan Rubens begged in obvious misery.

Anna tossed her head back, raised her chin, and spoke through her sobs, in a tone so impudent, that Maria cringed.

"Yes," she said, "Lord Rubens here is right. He is my lover—but a great man. So much finer than that awful Willem I am married to. And now that you know the worst, I beg of you to kill us both as quickly as possible."

A horrified look traveled across Jan Rubens's face, and he started to protest.

Onkel Jan looked at them both and spoke sternly, "You are both well worthy of death. You must make your plea to the husband you have wronged. Prince Willem will decide your fate. In the meantime, we have rooms for each of you in the dungeon."

Anna fell instantly to her knees and cried out, "No, do not ever make me go there. Kill me first, please, kill me first."

The guard pulled her to her feet and marched both prisoners off to the underground dungeon at the far end of the castle.

Oma muttered to Maria, "My Willem will never let them be killed."

In her heart, Maria knew Oma was right. But what would become of Mad Anna?

SPRING 1572

A year later, flowers once more covered the hillsides around the castle. The cherry trees bloomed, and the fields danced with daisies and poppies and wild irises—so many colors and so many different shapes of flower faces waving up at Maria as she walked back and forth to the herb garden each day. She was always tempted to linger longer than necessary in that sacred place where healing cures sprang from ancient soil.

Today she came here alone. Now sixteen, she'd been working with Oma and the herbs for five years. She knew so much about the plants and the ills that they repaired that she could do almost as much as Oma could.

When she'd completed her gathering for the day and her basket was filled to overflowing, she did not rush back to the castle. She wandered up and down the rows, soaking up the smells and the sounds of birds and breezes in the trees. Then she sat on the pondering bench where she could stare at the pear blossoms above her head and watch the bees flitting in and out gathering their nectar for the day.

Deep in thought about the wonders and beauties of this spot, she had no idea she was not alone until she heard an unfamiliar woman's voice: "Hello!"

Maria turned with a start and saw a plump middle-aged woman standing there, her head drooping slightly. Dressed like the wife of a merchant, she wore a shy, forced smile and curtsied.

"You live in the castle above?" she said hesitantly, in a voice not much louder than a whisper.

"Yes," Maria answered, standing quickly to her feet. "I was just gathering herbs for the day. Who are you? What brings you here?" She eyed the woman curiously. Rarely did a stranger come into the herb garden unannounced.

"I must see Count Willem . . . Prince van Oranje." She fingered the handle of the basket on her arm and stammered, "Y . . . you know . . . the man . . . I seek?"

"Yes." Maria chuckled. "I do know him." She watched the woman's nervous movements and the sparks of anxiety flashing in her dark eyes. "Why do you ask?"

The woman bit her lip, raised her head, and spoke with obvious effort. "B . . . because . . . Ach! . . . I simply must talk with the prince and I . . . I hope that perhaps you might help me . . . to find a way, quickly, to see him."

"Why is it so urgent that you talk with him?" Maria searched the stranger's face for a flicker of something that would tell her whether this woman was friend or foe.

She moved a step closer and, without looking directly at Maria, said, "I know I am a stranger to you. But the truth is, the prince and his mother and brother have been reading my letters now for the past year." She paused, then looked up guardedly. "They are the only ones who can help me, and . . . and I simply cannot wait longer for their answer."

Puzzled, Maria asked, "Hmm . . . Can you tell me what was the nature of your communication?"

The woman looked in every direction, as if needing to assure herself that no other ears were close by to hear her words. Then, drawing close to Maria, she spoke softly. "Um . . . you see, last year about this time, my husband was arrested and brought here in chains, along with the prince's estranged wife, Anna." She looked at Maria now with eyes like a frightened deer. "They say he was guilty of living with her, and that later she gave birth to his child."

"You are Jan Rubens's wife!" Maria's heart skipped a beat. How could she ever forget the pitiful memory of that man standing before Onkel Jan in the courtyard, his arms chained to a guard, his hair and clothes disheveled, pleading with Anna to speak the truth? She shuddered.

"Y. . .yes, I am his wife. Marie Pippelinck is my name."

"Did you believe the reports about your husband?" Maria looked at her with a mixture of pity and suspicion.

The woman stood for some time wringing her hands. "Yes, I believed the reports . . . bu . . . but I pleaded with the prince to show mercy on my poor, weak husband and to give him back to me!"

"I do not understand!" Maria said, not unkindly. "You know he has given his love to another woman, and yet you want him back?"

Slowly the stranger backed away a few steps. Then looking up into Maria's eyes, she pleaded once more, "Oh, my lady, Jan Rubens may be a weak man, but he is my husband. I have no one else to care for me and our child. We miss him, we need him . . . and, truly, he is a good man—not at all the way you may have come to think of him."

"Tell me about him," Maria invited, feeling strangely moved by this woman's pain.

"Oh! He is a gentle man, a kind man, a loving man."

Maria arched her eyebrows in a questioning glance. The woman moved closer again and reached out, grabbing Maria's arm with her hand. "Please try to see him as he really is, my lady. He is sometimes too loving . . . easily misled. And the woman who seduced him is ever so crafty and wily. Perhaps you already know that about her."

Maria said nothing but looked at the woman, wishing for all the world she could give her an herb to cure her sadness. "Oh," the woman pleaded, "if the prince would only release my Jan from prison, I would take him home once more, and I know he will never misbehave again."

"How do you know that? Has he written you so?"

"I know my husband, fair young woman. I know he has learned his lesson. Oh, can you help me take my plea to the merciful prince? I know he is merciful—otherwise my husband would already have been executed for his crime."

Maria looked at the round face before her, framed by the greenery of a linden tree. The woman's eyes swam with tears. Perhaps Maria should be mistrustful, but somewhere deep down inside, she believed the woman was sincere. In the end, Father must decide. If she spoke the truth, he would hear her plea and set the man free.

"I shall try," Maria said at last. "Come, follow me to the castle."

Marie Pippelinck clasped her hands together, and the beginnings of a smile danced across her face. Together the two women climbed the hill, and then Maria led the way directly to the chamber where she knew Father Willem sat in conference with his mother and Onkel Jan.

Leaving Marie Pippelinck outside the door, she entered cautiously. The minute she opened the door, all three people looked up at her.

"Forgive me, Father, that I interrupt you. But there is a woman here who is very anxious to speak to you. She insists the matter is quite urgent."

"Who is she and what does she want?" he asked, frown lines creasing his brow.

"She says her name is Marie Pippelinck and that you know her through the many letters she has sent to you this past year."

Father stretched back in his chair and tapped the table before him with his fingers. "Ah, yes, the wife! I have read her letters indeed."

"She promises that if you allow her to take her husband back home, he will never wander again. I told her I would ask if you are willing to speak with her."

Maria stood waiting, watching her father for some sign of which way he leaned. He continued tapping the table, saying nothing. Finally, he looked up at his mother, then back at Maria. "Send her in," he said.

"Would you like me to stay with you?" Oma asked.

"No, I think not," he answered. Then with a faint smile, he added, "I know your advice already." Maria pushed open the door, and she and Oma walked out into the sunshine. Oma gave the woman an encouraging smile and said, "I am Countess Juliana von Stolberg, lady of this castle. The prince will see you now."

Maria opened the door to let the woman in and watched her rearrange her skirts and headdress, patting them all into place. Then she walked in with a tense dignity that Maria knew was mixed with great fear.

"Oma," Maria said, when the woman had disappeared, "what will Father Willem tell her?"

"One can never say for sure," Oma said. "But I believe he will let the man go free. He's sat in prison now for a year and no doubt has had plenty of time to consider his misdeeds."

"And Anna? What will become of her?"

Oma shook her head and looked as grave as Oma could look with a mouth created always to smile. "Anna is a sick woman, my child. I fear she will live out her days in a dark and lonely dungeon of some sort, and probably die there, as well. It is a tragedy indeed."

PART 3

War:
A Battered Helmet and a Cause to Die For

1572–1574

Scarlet Oak Berry:

The Scarlet berry, made from red berries on the Scarlet Oak tree that grows profusely in Spain and other Mediterranean countries. Commended against the trembling and shakings of the heart, and swouning and melancholy passions, grief and sorrow . . . it is reported to recreate the minde and make a man merry and joyfull . . . for that it purgeth away melancholy humors.
—JOHN GERARD

15

AN ARMY FOR THE PRINCE OF ORANJE

29 JUNE 1572

The skies above the Dillenburg were a giant field of blue, filled with sheep-like clouds, tumbling from one horizon to the other. A brisk breeze moved them along and set the old castle flags whipping about their poles.

Maria, now sixteen, paused at the crest of the hill, in the shade of a spreading linden tree. She felt the breeze playing with her white starched headdress and tugging at her skirts, while she gazed out across the hillside and to the Dill River Valley below. There, alongside the river, lay a colorful encampment of army tents, stretching out beyond where she could see, around the bend. The uniformed figures moving this way and that, around the enclave, appeared almost as small as the toy soldiers her brother had played with when they were children in Breda.

"Banners billowing everywhere," she said aloud, speaking to no one. "Thousands of them—red and white and blue—and long orange ribbons fluttering over them all."

"Orange is our color, you know." A deep voice startled her.

"Ah, Father!" She looked up to see him seated on his brown horse. "I was so deep in thought, I did not hear you approach." How handsome he looked sitting astride his horse, just beyond the shade of the tree.

"I am the Prince van Oranje, you know," he said, smiling down at her.

"I do know it."

"And you are the Princess van Oranje, do not forget." He swung down from his horse and tethered the animal to a small white post beside a wooden bench beneath the tree. He came to stand with her and look at the sights below them.

Maria especially enjoyed these rare moments when she could have her father to herself for a little while. She wanted to make the conversation last as long as she could. "Your army is spread out in such colorful array," she said, "flying the flags, marching and shooting their guns, shouting and making loud clanging sounds. If I didn't know their warring purpose, I could find it almost beautiful."

For the past week, Maria had watched the men come in companies and set up their tents with pointed steeples. The whole valley had been transformed into a sea of moving people, animals, and guns. She had watched and listened—and wondered.

Father shook his head. "Yes, but it is not my army. It is the army of Oranje. These men are dedicated to the cause of the enslaved people of the Low Countries." He looked over the scene, then sighed and said, "How long I've known this day was coming—looked for it, prepared for it, prayed

142

for it to go well—and yet dreaded it. So many long hours I've spent with leaders of the resistance, making plans right here on this sacred spot." He gestured toward the tree.

Maria smiled. "What is so sacred about it? I remember playing here with Philips Willem on the rare occasions when we visited Oma here. We even chased each other into the tree once or twice."

Father smiled. "Ah, yes, and so did I. But this old tree now holds memories of a different sort for me."

"Memories of what, Father?" Maria asked.

Father Willem patted his horse on the flank, then walked under the tree's leafy branches and laid a hand on the trunk. "The first plans for this war were laid right here, on this very bench," he said.

"They were? When we first came from Breda to hide from your enemies?"

"Yes, that was the time. A group of leaders from the Low Countries came to me in great distress, begging me to help them force the iron-fisted Duke of Alva back to Spain."

"So that's why Ludwig and Adolf went to war?"

Father didn't look at her as he spoke. "And your Onkel Jan as well. Yes, that was the reason. Adolf sacrificed his life for our noble cause. Thank God, both Jan and Ludwig lived to return but . . ." He fell silent, but Maria could guess what was left unsaid.

"Will they go back again?"

"Yes, they will go again . . . and again . . . and yet again, as long as the enemy refuses to let our people rule themselves and worship as they believe . . ." Once more his words trailed off unfinished. He was staring at the army below and pondering in silence.

Finally, with a sad, quiet voice, he went on. "My brother Ludwig is a fine general. I've made him commander of all the forces of the Low Country resistance."

"But he is already on the battlefield, is he not? Will he come home to lead these troops assembled here?" Maria was puzzled.

"No. We have armies fighting in more than one place at a time. It works better that way, makes it harder for the enemy to destroy us."

"So, who will lead this army?"

Her father did not answer for a long moment. Maria stood by his side waiting. She sensed how difficult it was for him to talk about it. Finally he laid his hand across her shoulders and said softly. "It is my turn to go, my daughter."

"No!" she cried out, grabbing at his free arm. "No! They will kill you! You must not leave us!"

His shoulders sagged under a burden that seemed to get heavier as he stood there. Then slowly and carefully he said, "You must know, Maria, my daughter, that God has given to me a holy trust, a duty so important that I dare not leave it undone. If I do not go and help my people, they shall all be slaughtered, like so many pigs in a huge pen."

"They will?" Maria felt a shiver run up her back and down again.

"Yes, I fear that is true. Remember when King Philip and the Duke of Alva issued the statement that put the entire country under a death sentence?"

"Yes, Father." How could she forget?

"I suppose neither of them ever learned, as I did from my mother, that it is wrong to kill anyone simply because of what they believe. We must stop these men somehow." Father hung his head and worried a pebble with the toe of his shiny boot, then added soberly, "The mission is mine."

"But are you not afraid to go?"

"God goes with me," he said, his voice calm. "It is His cause and, whether I fear or not, I know He will keep me safe, as long as I do His bidding."

"Then what of Adolf? Was he not doing God's bidding? Is that why he died?"

"Maria, this is hard to learn, but sometimes only God knows what true safety is." Father took her in both arms and folded her tightly to his chest. "Since Adolf died, he is now safe in the arms of God. Nothing can harm him ever again, Maaike. Nothing."

Maria trembled in her father's arms. She felt a tiny trickle of warm tears on her cheeks and tasted their salt on her tongue.

"Father," she began at last, "Oma told me one time that she has a secret for staying happy, even when she is afraid."

" 'Trust God with everything'—is that what she told you?" Father asked, still holding her close.

"She's told you too, then?"

"Oma tells that secret to us all. She's spent her life learning to follow her own advice."

"But Father," Maria said, not quite sure how to say what was bursting in her heart, "I don't think I can trust God that much. Tell me how you do it. How you can go to war with these armies and not be afraid?"

For a long time, he held her and said nothing. At last, he released his embrace. Then, holding her by the arms, he looked into her eyes. She'd never seen this expression before. It penetrated deep into her soul the way her grandmother seemed to when she had something important to say.

"Maria," he said with quiet firmness, "no man can go to war without fear. Nor can we learn to trust God without going forward—even when great fear clutches at our hearts. I brought you here five years ago when all of our lives were in danger. I knew this was the way to protect us then. And I know that the Dillenburg is still the best place for you and my other children. I believe I can keep you safe here." He paused, still looking into her eyes.

"But I always knew God would one day call me to go back. It is my destiny from God, my reason for being born into this world. I truly believe that with my whole heart. And so I go. Am I afraid? Yes, very much afraid in some of the places deep inside of me. But, also, I go, expecting to learn to trust God in ways I've not yet had to trust."

"Oh Father, I am so afraid for you—for us all. I fear I shall never see you again. How can I watch you go?" Maria felt the pain of a whole war twisting like a sword in her heart. "I have lost so much already—first my mother, then our home in Breda, then Philips Willem, and a wagon load of family treasures sold to raise funds for the war. And now, you are going off to battle. Ach, it's too much! Too much!"

Father sighed. Maria watched him intently and saw a new light come on in his weary eyes. A smile played at the corners of his mouth.

"My daughter," he said at last, "can you trust your father to keep his word to you?"

Maria frowned, wondering what this meant. "Of course, I always trust you."

"Can you trust me now to do what I know is right?"

He paused and she pondered it. At last, she said lamely, "Yes, Father, of course I must, and I will."

"Good, because I must go where God calls me to go. I can do no other. I could promise you that one day I will either come back for you or send for you to join me wherever I am. But if a bullet should find me, I might not be able to keep that promise. So all I promise today is to love you always as my daughter, and to care for you and pray for you as long as God lends me breath. And I ask one thing of you."

"Anything, Father, anything."

"Promise me that when I leave you here tomorrow and go on my way you will pray every day. You will pray for me and for the success of the war and for safety in all the ways I go. You will also pray for my daughter, Maria—for strength to 'trust God with everything.' "

With his forefinger, Father lifted her chin. He smiled into her eyes and asked, "Can you promise me that, my Maaike?"

Maria swallowed hard and looked up at him. "Yes, Father, I promise to pray every day—for the war, for you, for me—and for Philips Willem." At the mention of his name, her fingers moved to the ruby hanging from her neck and she felt that awful pain again—the pain of saying good-bye to one's flesh and blood.

"Ah, yes," Father moaned, "and Philips Willem indeed."

She closed her eyes and felt him kiss her on the forehead. Then he was gone. He climbed on his horse and moved down the road toward his army—the army of the Low Countries— waving at her as he went. She waved back and watched him through misty eyes.

"Dear God," she prayed, "shall I begin today? Take care of my father and the war. Bring Philips Willem home. And help me trust You even when I am afraid."

16

A Very Present Help in Trouble

October 1573

Once Father led his troops away to the war in the Low Countries everything changed for Maria. She'd always worried about him when he was away on war business. But now that she'd seen his army camped down beside the Dill River, she could imagine him living with them in a battle tent, carrying a sword and a gun. Pictures of him riding his horse into battle followed her through every waking moment and sometimes far into the night.

Each day began, though, with one spot of peace, when Maria awoke to Toske's gentle touch on her shoulder and her familiar voice. "Good morning, Princess Maria. Time to be awake and greet the day."

Nobody else called her Princess, but it was a part of Toske's daily routine. This simple servant woman with the big heart helped her dress and braid her long blonde hair and tie it up under her white starched headdress. Maria loved those moments with the one woman who had always been with her, wherever she'd been. Toske was the only person in her life who never changed or went away.

They filled their morning time together with chatter about happy times remembered, beautiful things they were both learning, and dreams for Maria's future when she would be given to a fine nobleman and bear a houseful of happy children.

Then the first breakfast bell would sound, breaking the spell. Together, they would get down on their knees beside Maria's bed and offer the prayer she had promised Father she would pray.

"Dear Almighty God," she would begin. "Please, watch over my father with his troops. Bless this cause and bring peace and freedom to the people of the Low Countries. Protect Philips Willem, too, and bring him quickly home to us. And if You can, won't You teach me to trust You the way Oma does? Thank You. Amen."

Maria never heard Toske pray a prayer of her own, but she sensed her praying silently as they knelt side by side. Next, they rose and answered the second breakfast bell, moving out to face a world where things never went quite the way they wished or dreamed.

Maria went through the motions of her day. She struggled to find pleasure in daily things—the birth of a new colt, the antics of Meerkaatje and Hondje on their daily trips to the herb garden, the obvious joys of two servants in love, the beauties of a rose freshly bloomed, the wonder of a villager healed through their herbal attentions.

She had no enemies here—only friends. Aunts and uncles, cousins and classmates, and servants of a hundred sorts—they all treated her like an important part of their big family.

And, oh, those blessed hours with Oma and the herbs! It still filled her with awe.

But the uncertainties about Father dulled everything with a pale gray blur of anxiety. How could she ever forget that the Duke of Alva and every one of his soldiers carried Father's death sentence in their pockets and in their hearts? It prompted them every time they marched their horses or pointed their guns. She knew they thought of little else—and neither could she dismiss the thoughts, no matter how hard she tried.

At the end of every day, once again, Toske touched her with her magic. When she came to prepare her for bed, she would smile and laugh and make her feel loved and cared for—like a precious princess indeed.

Then came the fateful night when Maria returned to her room to find it dark and still. Toske had not lit her lamps or turned back the covers on her bed or laid out her nightdress.

"Toske," Maria called, then listened for an answer that did not come.

"Toske." She repeated her call, carrying the torch in her hand, into the corners of the room, in search of her. Toske was always here at this time of the night. Something had to be amiss.

Hurrying toward the low door at the far corner of the room, Maria shoved it open into Toske's tiny apartment. On the straw mattress of a bed in the corner, she found her sleeping. Maria knelt beside her and touched her forehead, then grabbed her by the hand.

"Toske!" she gasped, "You're burning with a fever!" Still no response. She held the torch close by and saw the mouth gaping, heard the breath coming in frightening gasps.

"Answer me, my Toske," she persisted until at last the woman moaned and reached for Maria's hand.

"Ach . . . didn't light your lamps," Toske mumbled and began pushing herself up on her left elbow. But she grimaced as if in pain and fell back instantly in silence.

Maria set her torch in a bracket on the wall and poured water from a pitcher into the washing bowl by Toske's bed. Grabbing a cloth, she dipped it in the water and washed the feverish forehead.

"Oh, my beloved Toske," she said again and again as she repeated the process. At last the woman's eyes began to flicker open and a faint smile appeared on the now-aging face.

"What happened, Toske?" Maria asked.

She breathed hard, then said weakly, "My arm . . . cut by . . . bramble vine."

"Show me," Maria said.

"Here," she mumbled, pointing to her right arm, "below . . . elbow." Maria pulled back the bed cover and shoved at the sleeve of Toske's garment. The woman winced and cried out in pain. Her arm was so swollen that Maria could not free it from the sleeve.

"Oh, Toske, no!" Maria gasped. "Why didn't you tell me so I could fix it earlier?"

"Ach, 'twas nothing," the woman answered lamely.

"Oh my! I'll go, right now, for my box of cures," Maria said. Gathering up her skirts, she stooped down and passed through the tiny doorway, returning quickly with the apothecary case Oma had helped her to assemble.

With a tiny knife she cut away Toske's sleeve so she could care for the swollen arm. The lump on the arm lay hot and tight in her hand.

"You have an angry green wound here," Maria said. How many of these wounds she had cleansed over the years since Oma had been teaching her the healing arts! But this time, she was working on her precious Toske. It had to go well. She could go for Oma, but why? She knew what to do.

"Almighty God," she prayed under her breath, "help me to do this right, and please save my dear friend."

"Toske, can you hear me?" she asked.

"Yes," came the faint reply.

"Thank God. Now, listen to what I say. I must pierce your wound with the knife and set all the nasty humors free. It will be painful."

"Already painful—and hot!" Toske mumbled.

"I know, I know. And when I've finished I shall cleanse it and put a crust of moldy bread on it till morning. Then I shall dress it with my mother's salve, and in a few days you will be as good as new."

A smile passed over the wan face lying on the mattress. "Oh yes!" She paused, breathed heavily, then added, "Anne's salve for green wounds."

With trembling heart and hands, Maria lanced the festering wound and drained it. Then she bathed it with fresh water and tied a crust of moldy bread on it. She spent the rest of the night bathing Toske's hot forehead in water.

Sometime before daybreak, the heat gave way to great beads of sweat. "Praise be to God," Maria cried out. "The cure is working." She wiped Toske's brow until the morning's sun burst through the single high window above the bed.

Toske opened her eyes. "You been here all night—with me?" she asked.

Maria smiled, leaned over, and kissed the no-longer fevered forehead. "My dear Toske, think how many nights you've spent with me when I was young, waiting on my needs. I am sure you must have bathed my hot forehead more than one night. This is my way of saying 'thank you.' "

With her well hand, Toske gripped Maria's and smiled up at her. The silence of her smile gave Maria the peace she needed to start one more day.

JANUARY 1574

On a cold, blustery day, when icicles hung from the ancient rafters and snowdrifts were piling up around the old creaky doors, the almost eighteen-year-old Maria sat with the rest of the family in the great hall of the Dillenburg. Wind whistled around the corner of the building and whipped at the enormous flag outside, all decorated with the roaring lion of the Nassau family coat of arms. A great fire crackled in the blackened fireplace that covered most of one end of the hall.

The girls and women tended to their embroidery and said very little. A handful of toddling children played with their dolls and tops and balls, while Meerkaatje scampered about among them. Their small voices chattered and sang and brought one bit of cheer to the cold, anxious atmosphere of the big room with ceilings reaching nearly to the heavens and draperies that only half covered tall glass windows.

Emilie, now five years old, leaned against Maria's leg. With obvious fascination she watched the needle move in and out of the cloth Maria held. The men sat huddled in one corner looking somber and talking in low tones.

No one said it, yet Maria knew that everyone knew it. Today was a fateful day in Juliana von Stolberg's family. Oma had five sons. Only three of them were with her today. Father Willem had left for the Low Countries a year and a half ago. And Onkel Adolf had died in battle so long ago Maria couldn't remember when it was. She was just a girl when it had happened and now, she was a woman.

Oma was looking down into her lap, concentrating on her sewing, when unexpectedly she mumbled, "Adolf should be with us." She sighed and smoothed out the embroidery work on her lap.

Maria had heard Oma say these same words repeatedly ever since he died. It was like she never quite forgot. *Was that the way it was to be a mother?* she pondered. She felt Emilie nudging her leg and thought again, *Unless you were like Mad Anna. Then you would never care.* Maria shivered. How hard it was to watch Oma when she looked so sad!

Today, her three remaining sons, Jan, Ludwig, and Hendrik, were dressed and prepared to walk out the door, into the snow, to join their brother Willem in the Low Countries.

Onkel Jan was leaving behind a wife and ten children of all ages—the oldest fourteen years and the youngest still a tiny babe in arms, barely a month old.

Onkel Ludwig was not married and so had neither wife nor children to leave behind. As the handsome commander of the armies in this war, he'd spent the early winter recruiting troops and now had come home for a few days to bid his mother and the rest of the family goodbye and to take his brothers off to the war.

Onkel Hendrik was Oma's youngest child, born just before her husband died. Only twenty-three years old, he'd already joined the others in battle several times in the past five years. He'd been excited to go again and talked about nothing else for weeks.

It was no secret to anyone in the castle that Oma didn't want Hendrik to go. When Ludwig first came home and announced his intentions to take him along, she'd asked, "Why must Hendrik go this time? He is so young. He has just recovered from a long feverish illness, you know, and the weather is nasty."

Maria felt a touch of fear in Oma's words. But she noticed that Ludwig's eyes seemed tender toward his mother when he spoke. He laid a hand on her shoulder and said gently, "I, too, have been ill, Mother. But we are both well now and the cause of religious freedom in the Low Countries needs our young blood."

Oma had smiled, but Maria knew that she was not happy with the idea. Nor was she herself happy with it. Night after night, Maria lay on her bed thinking about her father, wishing he would come home. Always she prayed, the way she'd promised Father she would, for God to protect him. Now she must pray, too, for her uncles as they went.

"I shall take good care of Hendrik for you, Mother," Ludwig promised. "He will fight many more battles before this war is finished—as must we all."

One more young man was going with them as well—Christoffel van de Paltz. Maria didn't know how it worked, but she'd been told he was their cousin. Like Hendrik, he was young and filled with enthusiasm for the cause. Maria watched his eyes sparkle. *How could these young men be so excited at the prospect of going to war?* she wondered. Father had told her that all men fear when they go to war. Surely that meant these uncles, too.

She tied a knot in her thread and felt a knot of another sort in her throat. Slowly, as if trying to calm some storm brewing within, she smoothed out the design of leaves on a meandering vine that followed the contour of the neck of a pale pink bodice. Emilie copied her motions and smoothed it with her chubby little hands, then looked up into Maria's face and said, "Beautiful! Sister Maria, will I someday be able to sew like you?"

"Oh yes, you will one day learn."

"Will you teach me?" she asked.

Maria remembered the day the servant had brought this child to the castle in a bundle of blankets. She thought about all the days since then—feeding her, clothing her, laughing and crying with her, trying to take the place of Emilie's absentee mother. Though she could never quite forget that the little girl was Anna's child, for some reason, she loved her almost as if she had been her own.

"Yes, Emilie," she said, smiling, patting the girl's hand. "I shall one day teach you to sew, and you will make finer garments than you have ever seen."

Suddenly the men began to stir. They stood to their feet, and Ludwig announced, "The time has come. We go!"

Maria's heart fluttered. She felt as if she were a wife seeing her husband off to battle, or a mother sending her sons into danger. A wave of sadness and fear swept over her.

"First," Oma spoke up from her place nearest the fire, "Jan will read to us from the Holy Book."

Onkel Jan walked to where a Bible lay on a stand and opened it somewhere near the middle. The whole family fell silent, children climbing into laps of the adults, and Hendrik corralling the monkey in his arms.

"God is our Refuge and strength," Onkel Jan read. "A very present help in trouble."

Do they really believe that? Maria wrinkled her brow and listened with questions piercing her heart. Jan went on:

> Therefore we will not fear, though the earth should change,
> And though the mountains slip into the heart of the sea;
> Though its waters roar and foam,
> Though the mountains quake at its swelling pride.

Maria looked at the faces around the room. Perfectly blank, they were. No one smiled, no one frowned. She wondered how many were hiding the kinds of fear she felt deep in her heart at this moment. But there was more. "Come, behold the works of the Lord," Onkel Jan read on.

> Who has wrought desolations in the earth.
> He makes wars to cease to the end of the earth;
> He breaks the bow and cuts the spear in two;
> He burns the chariots with fire.
> Be still and know that I am God;
> I will be exalted among the nations, I will be exalted in the earth.
> The Lord of hosts is with us;
> The God of Jacob is our stronghold!*

* Psalm 46:1–3, 8–11 (v. 10 is from the NIV)

Jan closed the big Bible and said without looking up, "We go in the strength of these words, 'Our God is a very present help in times of trouble.'"

Maria held her breath and gathered Emilie close. Did they all trust as much as Onkel Jan said he did? Was this maybe one of the moments when Oma found it hard to trust, too?

Oma stood to her feet, then motioned for them to bow their heads.

"Dear Almighty God," she prayed, "we cry out to You to have grace and mercy upon these our sons. You have called them to go to war, to win for Your people the freedom to worship You in spirit and in truth, to bring an end to the horrible slaughter of people because of their beliefs. We ask You to recall the promises from this Your Word. Keep these men of ours, in all their ways, that they may never cease to trust in You and in Your goodness. Protect them from all evil and give them a long and fruitful life. In the powerful name of Jesus, our King, Amen."

Ludwig walked to where Oma stood, hugged her, and kissed her cheek and smiled. "Thank you, Mother," he said. "I shall be back as soon as God has given the enemy into our hands and brought the Low Countries under the control of her own people."

She gathered her sons around her then, hugging each one, and reminding them, "Whatever happens, never cease to trust the Almighty!"

"With everything," they all added in chorus.

"With everything indeed!" Oma smiled.

Maria listened and watched and pulled Emilie closer. She tried to still the terrible questions that taunted her. What if the men didn't come back after all? And what if Father Willem also didn't come back? What could she tell Emilie? And how could she ever again believe in this God who wrote the promises Onkel Jan had just read from His book?

The men moved out through the door, into the wind and cold snow. Emilie got down from Maria's lap and ran to the window to watch them go. Maria watched her breathing on the icy windowpane, trying to thaw a spot clear. She heard the sounds of horses being reined in, the muffled clopping of hooves through the snow onto the cobblestones. She returned to her sewing, but her mind paid attention only to the sounds outside as the hounds began to howl.

Emilie tugged at her skirts and asked, "When will they come back?"

Maria opened her mouth, but her heart pounded so hard she could scarcely breathe. What could she say?

From the window, where Oma stood, wiping a spot clear of frosty cold, they all heard an answer, "When God wills it, they will be home."

17

MY SOUL WAITS
IN SILENCE

MAY 1574

February's snow continued to pile up around the castle grounds and sadness and worry hovered in every drafty old room. Occasionally a messenger arrived with some tidbit of news. A battle had been won, a battle had been lost, a city had surrendered, a visitor was coming.

Life went on, a dull blur of duties and apprehension. Five meals a day were prepared and served in the dining hall. Horses were fed and shoed. Children were cared for. Classes were taught in the court school. Servants cleaned and washed clothes and laid fresh rushes on the floors and collected eggs in the hen houses. Oma went about her duties, caring for her servants and her grandchildren and supervising all else that went on. But Maria saw sadness in her eyes, felt it in her weary voice, watched it in the slowing of her steps as she walked about the castle and up and down the hill, taking herbal cures to the villagers.

Spring came at last, bringing flowers, sunshine, and showers, and bright green leaves on the trees. But the days felt longer than usual, and the flowers didn't look half so bright as in past years.

One day Onkel Jan trudged up the hill and through the gates. The whole family gathered around him to hear the latest news. But when he told his story, they could only weep.

"I was with the army, heading north. We planned to join Willem and his troops for a large battle. But Ludwig's troops were angry. We had not had enough money to pay them their wages for some time, and they were refusing to fight one more day without it.

"So, Ludwig sent me back to Cologne to see if I could find someone to lend us more money. Two days after I left, on a wide field of heather called Mook Heide, the Spaniards attacked our army by surprise. Still grumbling about the lack of wages, Ludwig's men didn't follow orders well. I was not there to see the awful sight. I only know I heard the word from a few men who barely escaped with their lives.

"The Spaniards scattered and trampled on them. They followed those who fled to the nearby river and drowned them in the water. Some of our soldiers took refuge in farmhouses, which the Spaniards burned to the ground with all the men inside."

Onkel Jan did not look at his mother, and Maria knew that Ludwig and Hendrik had met with disaster.

"What of my sons?" Oma asked at last.

Jan hung his head. "They are still out there somewhere. They would not give up the fight, that much I know."

Oma grabbed Jan by the arm and asked, "But you have not seen them or heard from them, have you?"

"I was not there, Mother." He patted her arm with his big hand. "In time, we shall hear."

Maria cried herself to sleep that night. She wondered how many other people in the castle did the same.

19 June 1574

In the middle of a drizzly summer day, Maria was so terribly sad she didn't know what to do with herself.

Ludwig and Hendrik had disappeared in battle well over a month ago. Everybody in the family—and all their servants—knew that the two men were never coming home again. They felt it in their bones. Still not a word had come. After such a long time, only a miracle could save them now.

Oma expected that miracle every day. She simply would not believe that they were gone. She tried to talk cheerfully about the day when they would come home. She had her servants take special care to keep the men's rooms clean and ready for their return.

And because Oma was so insistent, nobody else would speak against it. Maria didn't know quite why, but it seemed to her that if they could just talk about it, she might feel a little better. Worst of all, she worried day and night about Father Willem. Maybe nobody else did, but she couldn't stop thinking about him. Was he out on a battlefield somewhere? Had somebody come up behind him when he was not looking and shot him in the back? Did he have enough food to eat, a warm place to sleep?

Then, as always happened whenever she worried about anything, she began thinking about her brother and adding him to her list of worries. She hadn't seen him or heard a word about him since the duke kidnapped him, way back when she was only twelve years old and he was thirteen. What did he look like now, at nearly twenty? Were the Spaniards kind to him? Did they try to turn him against Father Willem and the family? If he could come to live at the Dillenburg, would he still be her close friend?

By the time the noon meal was over, Maria's heart was so filled with pain and thoughts she could not control that she simply had to find a place where she could kneel and pray. Normally she ran to the pondering bench in the garden, but today it was being pounded by rain. For a while, she wandered aimlessly up and down the corridors of the old drafty castle and hoped not to meet anyone she'd have to talk to.

That's when she remembered the chapel. Ah, yes, it would make a fine place of quiet refuge. She hurried there and nudged at one of the huge old doors with her shoulder. It creaked so loudly that she jumped with a start.

She tiptoed inside the tiny, dimly lit room with its simple stained glass windows and high ceilings. A few rows of short benches with attached kneeling rails beckoned to her. With its dark wood walls and benches, and with clouds outside that kept the sunlight from shining through the windows, the room was gloomy, cool, and damp.

Feeling as if she were entering a mysterious cave, she walked to the back corner of the room and knelt on a kneeling bench.

"Almighty God," she began, her voice sounding strange and far away in her ears, "do you know where my father is? And Onkels Ludwig and Hendrik, and Cousin Christoffel? I've never seen a war and hope I never have to. I know people die there from gunshots and sword thrusts and from being trampled by horses."

She looked up at the front of the chapel, expecting to see a painting of Jesus looking down at her. But the wall and altar were both bare. The decorations from the chapel were among the many things sold to pay for the war.

"Great God, why can You not stop this ugly war?" she cried out. Then all fell silent except for her deep, painful sobs and the splashing of raindrops on the windowpanes.

How long she knelt there weeping, worrying, trying to pray, she had no idea. But at last she heard an enormous creaking sound. The door was opening! She heard a shuffling of feet in the rushes, then saw, through the gloomy light, someone rushing down the aisle to the front row of seats and flinging herself on a kneeling bench. Then came a burst of loud howling.

Maria froze in her place. Should she leave? Somehow, she didn't think she could move, so she stayed kneeling, waiting, terrified by the grief of the woman who had joined her in this solitary place.

"Almighty God in the heavens," came the words through the woman's tears.

Oma! Maria gasped, and clapped her hand over her mouth. She'd never heard Oma cry like this before. Always so strong and brave and with the mouth that never frowned—No, it couldn't be Oma! But it was. Maria knew the voice.

"Willem has written to me, oh, God."

Father Willem has written? Then he, at least, must be alive! Relief mixed with sorrow and left Maria trembling. She pulled her cloak tightly around her body and tried to calm her spirit.

"He says Ludwig and Hendrik are dead!" Oma gasped. "Must I believe it? Give me a sign—that I may know!"

Oma began to wail, gigantic waves of grief heaving up from the bottom of her soul. "My Lord, my Lord—I am distraught and overcome with great grief. Willem tells me that You in Your grace will never allow anything to happen that is not Your will. How can he say that today?"

On and on it went, wailing and moaning and crying such as Maria had never heard from anyone before.

Should she go to Oma and try to console her? Maria remembered how many times, over the years, Oma had helped dry her tears. But now, when she thought to step forward, something stopped her. Oma, after all, didn't know she was here. She, like Maria, had come here to be alone. Maria continued to kneel with hands folded, eyes closed.

For God only knew how long, she continued to hear Oma cry her heart out. Here and there the sobs stopped long enough for a few words of agonizing prayer:

"I taught Willem those words he wrote about You, God . . . I was not grieving then . . . True words, that my soul knows right well . . . But today they pierce my soul and leave me in a pool of blood."

Enough! Maria could not stay. She rose to her feet and moved toward the door. Solitude was the only gift she could give her dear grandmother. She cringed as the door squeaked.

"Don't let her hear it, God," she prayed. "She must never know I was here with her."

But before she could close the door, she heard Oma's voice clear and controlled, reciting a Bible verse she'd heard from her many times before:

My soul waits in silence for God only . . .
*I shall not be greatly shaken.**

Maria latched the door and hurried down the corridor, the words ringing in her ears, "My soul waits in silence."

If Oma has a secret source of strength, that must be it. Maria told herself. "Great God, I want to be as strong as she is."

---

* Psalm 62:1–2.

18

WHEN I AM AFRAID

20 JUNE 1574

No matter how heavy her mood, Maria loved the morning after a storm. There was no better time to go gathering herbs. The garden was alive with fragrance and colors and birdsongs. Remnants of yesterday's rain lay in sparkling little droplets on the leaves.

Oma and Maria took Emilie with them into the garden today. Emilie carried Meerkaatje, and Oma and Maria carried the baskets and knives for clipping the herbs. As usual, Hondje scampered at their feet, brushing his tail against their skirts, sniffing out all the little pockets of damp earth and bugs that crawled around after a summer rain.

" 'This is the day that the Lord has made,' " Oma said, obviously trying to be her normal cheerful self. Maria knew full well that her grandmother's tone of voice was no more than a brave façade. Just yesterday afternoon, she'd heard her wailing in the chapel and even now she heard heavy overtones in the older woman's voice.

Oma patted Emilie's shoulder and added the rest of her Bible verse, " 'We will rejoice and be glad in it.' "

Emilie looked up and smiled. "What's 'joice, Oma?"

"Oh, Emilie, rejoice is what we do when we laugh and sing because Jesus puts joy in our hearts," Oma said, but she couldn't hide the sigh that followed her words.

Emilie laughed. She grabbed Meerkaatje's paws, one in each hand, and clapped them together. " 'Joice, Meerkaatje, 'joice!" she said, then laughed again. The monkey pulled free and scampered away amongst the profusion of greenery.

Maria didn't feel quite ready to rejoice this morning herself. Yesterday's clouds would hang in the corners of her soul for a long time to come. Not even for Emilie's sake could she try to make it sound as if the sun had chased all the clouds away.

"Good girl," Oma said. "And now we cut the herbs and you and Meerkaatje and Hondje play."

They had scarcely begun their work for the morning, when she heard the sound of hunting hounds up by the castle. Maria was bent over a fragrant bush of rosemary. She rose up and looked to the roadway. A lone figure on a horse, carrying bags, galloped up the hill. Suddenly he stopped and veered off down the pathway that led to the herb garden.

"Who is our visitor, Oma?" Maria asked.

Oma straightened and raised her hand to her forehead to shield her eyes from the sun. "Ah, that is my old courier friend, Pieter-Lucas, with the long golden curls." She stopped, then went on a bit more somberly, "He always brings news from the Low Countries."

Maria's heart beat rapidly. *If he has news from the war, why is he bringing it out here to Oma in her garden? Should he not take it first to*

Onkel Jan? Fear knotted her stomach. She reached instinctively for Emilie as if to protect her.

"Hallo! My honorable Countess Juliana," the young man called from his horse. He reigned in just outside the garden hedge, and Oma rushed to his side.

"What news do you bring this day, young Pieter-Lucas?" Oma asked. The fragile tone of cheer and "rejoicing" had vanished from her voice. "Have you found my sons?"

The messenger didn't answer. He fumbled with his bags, then he pulled out a mysterious object. He seemed nervous as he held it out to her. About twice the size of his head, it was a huge lump of charred metal. "I'm sorry to say it, Countess, but I fear this is all we have found." He spoke gently, as if she were his mother, Maria thought. But in the silence that followed, she seemed to hear the words unspoken, inside Pieter-Lucas's mind, "It is all we will ever find."

"What is it?" Oma asked.

He did not answer, but put the object in her hands. She ran her fingers over its battle-scarred contours. From where Maria stood just inside the hedge, she could see it was pocked with dents and sharp protrusions and holes, and had tattered remains of a leather strap barely attached.

"A metal helmet!" Oma gasped. "Ludwig! No, not Ludwig!"

Pieter-Lucas took it from her and turned it over. In a silence so deep it seemed to stop even the birds from singing, they watched him probe the hollow space that had once protected a man's head. From the crown of the battered helmet, inside what remained of the leather lining, he extracted a worn scrap of paper and placed it in her hand.

"He left you a message, Countess," Pieter-Lucas said softly.

The yellowed paper was tattered at the edges, splattered with dark stains. Blood? The paper's creases were so worn that light shown through in places.

"Ach!" Oma said, breathing out her words like an enormous sigh. "I wrote this letter with my own hand. I sealed it with my own sealing wax!" She stared at the letter, her mouth sagging open.

"Almighty God, it cannot be!"

She began to read in a mumbling voice, as if piecing together sweat-smudged words, barely readable on patches of paper that had worn almost away to nothing:

"Dearly beloved son, I send you herewith a short prayer and ask you to pray it every day and to beg for God's compassions in all your circumstances . . ." She stopped and wiped at her eyes with the back of her sleeve. ". . . that He may guard you against all evil and may lead you on the way that is well-pleasing to Him and keep you always in His divine protection."

Nothing stirred and no one spoke for a long time. Oma stood weeping, her fingers caressing this precious piece of her own soul that had become a part of her son's soul as well. At last, she read the final lines, "I will also pray for you diligently; don't you, either, grow careless in prayer. Dillenburg, the last of August 1566. Your always faithful Mother, Juliana Countess of Nassau, Widow."

Without looking up she pondered aloud, "And he carried it with him always, these eight years—to the death?"

"My Lady," Pieter-Lucas offered, "more than once, I watched your son pull it from his helmet and read its contents. And always when he finished it, he bowed his head and prayed."

"Ach, God!" she mumbled, looking at no one.

Then, ignoring the rest of them, Oma began to walk up the pathway. Pieter-Lucas walked his horse behind her in respectful silence. Emilie tugged at Maria's hand and said, "Oma's not 'joicing, Sister Maria."

The herb garden turned misty before Maria's eyes. She squeezed the little hand that clung to hers and urged, "Come, let us go home." She busied herself gathering up baskets and the animals. "Hold tightly to Meerkaatje," she told Emilie.

Together they trudged along behind Oma and Pieter-Lucas, up the sunny pathway and the road and through the inner castle gate. Here the procession came to a standstill, when Oma stopped, turned, and spread wide her arms toward the blue, blue sky.

"My soul waits in silence for God only," she cried aloud. "What time I am afraid, I will put my trust in Thee, Almighty God. I shall not be greatly shaken. Amen."

Maria turned to her tiny half-sister, and knelt down to hug the child close. "Someday soon," Maria whispered, "Oma will 'joice again."

23 JUNE 1574

For the next two days, Oma scarcely talked with anyone. She came to meals, and nothing more. Maria gathered herbs alone, or with Emilie. Daily, she mixed healing recipes in the apotheek and took Emilie with her to the village at the foot of the hill where they visited Oma's patients.

Then on a warm and sunny morning, Maria decided what she could do for Oma to make her feel better. She slipped into the apotheek right after breakfast and began going through the recipes and books piled on the shelf beneath the windows. Surely somewhere among them she could find instructions for making a healing potion to cure a sorrowful broken heart. She knew all about borage, which was especially helpful when boiled in wine. But that was only good for minor sorrows and melancholy spirits. Oma needed a stronger cure.

She searched through a seemingly endless pile of old yellowed sheets of paper with fading ink scrawls until she came upon one little note that offered a ray of hope. Penned in a handwriting she did not recognize, it read: "The Scarlet Berry, made from red berries on the Scarlet Oak tree that grows profusely in Spain and other Mediterranean countries. Recommended for use against the trembling and shaking of the heart, and melancholy diseases, grief and sorrow. It is reported to restore the mind and make a man or woman merry and joyful."

"Where might I find some scarlet oak berries?" Maria asked herself. She searched the bottles and boxes and baskets and hanging dried branches and sprays. She had no memory of seeing such a thing here. But why would Oma keep the recipe if she didn't have the ingredients needed to make it?

She had searched the last corner when the door to the room opened and in walked Oma. Her shoulders drooped slightly. When her eyes met Maria's, the older lady smiled a weak smile and said, "Aha, I find you hard at work among our precious herbs. What is the recipe you study there?"

"Oh, Oma, good morning," Maria said, wondering what to say next. "I have missed you these days and am so happy to see you back."

Oma had walked to the table where the recipes were spread about, and she stood staring at the one Maria had placed on top of the pile. For a long while, she said nothing. At last, she said in a gloomy tone, "Every herbalist at some time or another searches for a remedy among her miracle-working substances and plants to heal a broken heart."

"You have done the same?" Maria asked, hesitantly.

Oma sighed. "Ah yes, my Maaike. I too have looked at the Scarlet Berry recipe and wished the Scarlet Oak that bears them grew in these parts, where we could experiment with it. So many sorrowing people all around us." She shook her head, then approached Maria.

"Then you have not tried it?" Maria asked.

Oma laid a hand on her shoulder and said, "No, I have only dreamed. I cannot bring myself to discard the recipe, which was here in the apotheek when I first moved into the Dillenburg. A former lady of the castle must have had the same dreams as you and I."

Maria looked carefully at her grandmother, searching for some clue about her state of mind, but Oma would not look her in the eye. "Oma, tell me," Maria asked, "what medicine do you give, when borage is not enough, to restore a patient to happiness?"

Oma smiled and took Maria by both hands. "Only two things I have found over the years, and you will not see them in these shelves."

"Not here? Where then?"

Still holding tightly to both of Maria's hands, Oma said gently, "One is a gift God has given to us all—the gift of time. Day after day, as we get farther and farther from the sad events that make us grieve, we feel ourselves stronger and stronger."

Maria opened her mouth to ask how much time it would take for Oma to be well again, but she could not speak. Instead she listened as Oma went on.

"The second part of the recipe, you have heard from me many times before. It is a common ingredient."

"Oh?" Maria stared at her and saw the beginnings of a twinkle in the old gray eyes.

"Those four little words . . ." Oma paused.

"Trust God with everything?" Maria asked and almost wished she'd held her peace and let Oma say it.

"That is it! You learn well."

"But, Oma," Maria began, choosing her words with care, "what of the days when you cannot trust, when you do not want to trust, when the pain grows greater than the trust?" Somehow she knew those were the kind of days Oma was passing through, and she had to know how to endure them.

Oma tugged her to a chair by the window where the morning sun streamed through. They sat and let it warm them. "That, Maaike, is where we must let time do its work in us. I . . . I know what it is like to grieve and feel as if you will never see the sun shine one more day. You know that you have always trusted God from as far back as you can remember and you know in your heart of hearts that He can be trusted. But you feel totally overwhelmed by the grief." Maria watched as Oma struggled to go on. She wiped at her eyes. Maria laid a hand on her grandmother's old, wrinkled hand and tried to think of something comforting to say. Nothing came.

With obvious effort, Oma went on, nodding as she talked. "Oh, yes, Maaike, that is the most important time to stop and wait for time to do its healing work."

"You just sit in your chair and wait?"

"Sometimes you do that for a while. Otherwise, you go on and eat your meals and give your servants their orders and do your daily work, because others depend on you to keep things moving. But you spend time trying, at least, to read God's book—to fill your mind with His promises."

"But Oma, He doesn't always keep the promises Onkel Jan reads to us."

Oma looked at her, startled. "Oh?"

"No, He doesn't. Remember before Onkels Ludwig and Hendrik left, with our cousin Christoffel, remember what Onkel Jan read that day?"

Ach, what would Oma think of her now? Oma had lost her sons, but it was Maria who was losing her faith.

"Tell me, what did he read that day?" Oma stared out the window, and her voice sounded far away.

Maria scrambled to remember the words. "I don't remember all of it, just the important part—something like, 'God is our refuge and strength and helps us when we get into trouble.' "

Oma nodded. "Yes, that was the promise I reminded God about every day after my boys left home."

"Then what did He tell you when they didn't come back?" Maria asked.

"He told me to read the promises over and over and then said, 'Trust me, my child. I will not abandon your sons, not now or ever!' "

"Then what happened when Pieter-Lucas came—with the helmet? What did God say to you on that day?" Maria sat waiting, her heart beating so fast, it felt as if it might burst through her chest.

Oma was silent. She and Maria clung to each other's hands, and it felt almost as if they spoke through their touch. Maria began to feel stronger, not quite so worried. What was in this woman who had so much grief of her own needing to be healed, that allowed her to pour new strength into Maria?

"The ways of Almighty God are very difficult to understand," Oma said at last. "When He says He will protect, He does protect."

"Then why did He let Ludwig and Hendrik be killed in battle? What kind of protection is that?"

"I know, Maaike, I know." Oma paused and soon Maria heard Oma's breath coming in deep, slow heaves. "When my heart is heavy, I, too, struggle to believe. Remember, I have told you that before."

"Then you no longer believe and trust in God?" Maria knew that if Oma could not believe, neither could she believe.

"Oh, my Maaike, how can I explain to you the ways of faith?" Oma was holding both of Maria's hands in her own now, stroking them, and smiling through tear-filled eyes. "God has taken both of my sons to heaven. They are not dead, but more alive than ever they could have been on this earth. Nothing can harm them again, Maaike, nothing!"

Maria gasped. "That's what Father said about Onkel Adolf."

Oma smiled and nodded. "Ah yes, Adolf too, and both of my loving husbands and my parents and the babies I lost and the friends. I cannot explain it better. I only know that when God allows one of His children to die here on this earth, He takes them to a new and better life."

"Oh, Oma," Maria said aloud, "when I grow to be an old woman, I want to be just like you. And until then, I want never to leave you—never!"

Suddenly, Oma was hugging her in strong arms. Maria wished they might stay this way forever. If only Duchess Margaretha could have really known Oma, she never would have said the fearful things she said back there in the court of Brussels. The warnings that woman had filled her head with all seemed so ridiculous now.

"When I am afraid," Oma mumbled into Maria's padded shoulders. Maria joined her on the last phrase, "I will put my trust in God." She had no idea how or when, but Maria now had hope that the day would come when she, too, could trust God with everything.

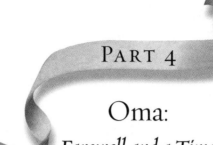

PART 4

Oma:
Farewell and a Time for Moving On
1577–1580

Rosemary:

This herbe is hote and dry. Take the flowers and put them in a lynen clothe & so boyle them in fayre clene water to ye halfe & coole it & drynke it for it is moche worth against all euylles in the body. —BANCKES'S HERBALL, 1525

As for Rosmarine, I lett it runne all over my garden walls, not onlie because my bees love it, but because it is the herb sacred to remembrance, and, therefore, to friendship; whence a sprig of it hath a dumb language that maketh the chosen emblem of our funeral wakes and our buriall grounds. —SIR THOMAS MORE

Speaking of the powers of rosemary, it overtoppeth all the flowers in the garden . . . It helpeth the brain, strengtheneth the memorie, and is very medicinable for the head. Another property of the rosemary is, it affects the heart. Let this rosmarinus, this flower of men ensigne of your wisdom, love and loyaltie, be carried not only in your hands, but in your hearts and heads. —ROGER HACKET, D.D. (1607 SERMON)

19

Your Father's Daughter

25 August 1577

Dusk fell softly over the Dillenburg, a golden glow from the fading light in the summer sky reaching into the stone-enclosed corridors, arcades, and high-ceilinged rooms. Maria, now a young lady of twenty-one years, stood at the door of Oma's bedroom with an alabaster flask of rosemary tonic in her hand. She listened to the clock in the tower of the chapel sounding its eight long bells. Officially the day had ended.

For many years this had been the signal for Oma to move about among her beloved servants and castle residents. She had personally served them a soothing drink called a nightcap and wished them each a pleasant night. Then they scattered to their quarters, either in the village or throughout the castle. Finally, Onkel Jan carried his ringful of jangly keys to the palace gates where he locked them for the night and then escorted his mother to her apartment on the far side of the castle square.

But those days were gone. Oma was now old—past her seventieth year. Elizabeth, Onkel Jan's wife, had taken her place and now served the traditional nightcap. Maria watched her aunt and uncle move off to their duties, then raised her hand to knock on Oma's door. But instead of knocking, she paused and looked around her.

Not only had the day ended, so had her time in this wonderful place. Tomorrow she must go away. Her father had brought her here. Now he had sent for her, and she must go to him. She breathed in deeply, trying to gather up all the Dillenburg air she could hold to take with her on the long journey that lay ahead.

How strange to recall that when she came here she was full of fear. Demons and Bibles and heretics threatened her in her nightmares. And now none of those things troubled her any more. She could think of no place on earth so peaceful and happy as the Dillenburg. It had been her home for ten years—the happiest years of her life. She gazed fondly at the old buildings, the flag with the Nassau lion, the tower, the hall that led to her beloved apotheek. Then she looked off toward the hill and thought of the herb garden, that sanctuary of all sanctuaries where she had spent numberless hours, getting to know Oma and the herbs—and God.

Trying to calm the racing of her thoughts and feelings, she leaned against the old door and ran her fingers over its splintery wooden surface. How she loved this place and the old woman on the other side of this door! Could she bring herself to climb into Onkel Jan's coach tomorrow morning, along with Anna's children, little Anna and Maurits—oh yes, and Toske, dear Toske? Ach, but they must leave Oma behind, along with

Emilie and other family members she loved—to head for the Low Countries and a reunion with Father Willem.

"But I will return," she told herself in a whisper. She knew Father was anxious for her to meet his new wife Charlotte, her new stepmother—how that word still struck terror into her heart. There were also Charlotte's two infant daughters. And possibly Maria would be needed to help to settle the new household. Hopefully, Father didn't have a marriage in mind for her—not yet. For Oma still needed her. Later? Ah yes! At twenty-one, she did think about it often. But for now . . . how she wanted to come back here to be with Oma and nurse her through her final days! Surely it would not be long!

Gently she knocked on the door she had passed through so many times. A familiar voice, now shaky and muffled, reached her through the weathered wood.

"Come in, Maaike." The words shone like golden sunrays in the shadowy places of her mind.

She found Oma sitting propped up in her enormous four-poster bed with the crenellated silk curtains. Her smile reached out, and Maria hurried to plant a kiss on an old wrinkled cheek. Oma's spindly hand grasped hers, and the two looked intently at each other for a long and beautiful moment.

"I've come to give you your rosemary tonic," Maria said at last, "and read to you from the Bible you taught me to love." She released herself from the handclasp, then removed the cork from the flask she held and put it into Oma's outstretched hand.

"Ah, thank you, my dear nursemaid," Oma said. She slowly swallowed down the contents of the bottle. "You are an angel of God's mercy, you know."

Maria blushed as she took the flask and rearranged the pillows and blankets around her grandmother. How she would miss these tender moments, making Oma as comfortable as possible!

"I am looking about this room with its ancient tables and chairs and chests," Oma said aloud in a dreamy tone of voice, "and seeing many things from my past."

"What kinds of things?" Maria asked, still fluffing pillows and tucking in feather beds.

"For twenty-eight long years, I shared this room with Willem the Elder, your grandfather, whom you scarcely knew. What a pity! He was a gentle man with a kind face, a generous spirit, and a determined nature. A faithful husband, a good father, and a respected nobleman among the noblemen of Germany. I often think I can feel him here with me yet." She stared off into the space beyond Maria's shoulder and smiled.

"I have had a good life here in this place," she added.

"I know that, Oma," Maria said, "and so have I. I have no desire to leave you. To go and live with my father and his new family? Well, yes, I do want to be with Father, but . . ." So much was better left unsaid.

"Ah, my child, this wife that God has given to your father is as lovely and loving a woman as you will ever find on earth." Oma looked at the golden band on her wrist and smiled up into Maria's face. "Every time I look at this bracelet that she gave to me, I remember her kind words in the letters she has written, and I can only give thanks to God for her. I still wish one day to meet her face to face."

"You shall have that joy someday, Oma," Maria said, wanting it to be true, yet not at all certain she believed either that the meeting would take place or that Charlotte could possibly be all that she seemed in her letters.

"When I think of all the horrible years my son spent with that mad Anna . . ." Oma shook her head and sighed. "Oh my, but those were dreadful times! How hateful she was to him—always caring only for herself. In the midst of his worry and overwhelming responsibility, he so desperately needed a woman to love him and look after him, to care about his good, and to try to lighten his burdens."

"And you think Charlotte is that sort of woman, Oma?"

The smile that spread across the wrinkled face shone with joy. "Ah, yes, I have no doubt of it. Nor should you, Maaike. You have read her letters, translating them from Charlotte's mother tongue, French, for this old country woman who never learned the language of letters. So what think you?"

"It does indeed appear that she is everything my father might ever want or need in a wife. When I read his letters, I know that he is more happy than I've ever known him to be." Maria paused while her thoughts tumbled about looking for a way to come out in a sensible order. "It's just that . . ."

"It's just that what?" Oma asked, then without waiting for an answer rushed on. "Of course I would like to keep you here with me. But I rejoice that you can be a part of such a good and loving family, my Maaike."

"But Oma," Maria protested, "you need me here so badly." She could remind Oma about how in her growing blindness she needed daily help with the reading and the writing of letters, with walking around, with the apotheek, with a hundred other things. Or she could mention Oma's loneliness that Maria so often cured with her presence. For in her old age, especially since the loss of her sons, Oma seemed to have an almost constant sadness of spirit, one that Maria loved to cheer.

But Maria did not say any of it. What good would it do to remind her grandmother of such sad things on this, their last night together?

"I know," Oma said, "I think at times that I cannot live without you beside me. And I have told my son so. For some reason, he seems not to hear me."

"Nor does he listen to my pleas or Onkel Jan's. Why?"

Oma sighed. "You know, Maaike, I am only his aging mother. I cannot see inside of him to know what makes him all he is today. I only know he is a wise man and a loving son, and he will always have his reasons. I would never want to withhold from him whatever joy you might bring to him with your presence in his first real home."

"But Oma—" Maria began. Oma shook her head and put her hand over Maria's mouth. "Think a moment with me," she said. "You are his daughter, not mine. Not since your mother died when you were two years old has he had a complete family. Finally now he feels he can shelter you in a safe home. And God knows, with his enemies hard on his heels every moment, he may not have many days left to spend with his daughter either."

"Oh, Oma." Maria was sitting on the bed beside her grandmother now, holding both her spindly old arms. For a long while, the two women gazed deeply into each other's eyes. Maria saw the film across Oma's eyes, and yet she felt them piercing into the innermost part of her being. Oma had always been able to go to that place in her, whenever she chose.

Maria reached to the table by the bedside for Oma's Bible. "I remember the day I first saw this Bible," Maria said. "Down in the village, at the home of the butcher. You took it out of your apotheek case and read from it. The butcher's wife and all her children listened intently, and I was horrified. I expected to see demons spring from its pages and gobble up those unsuspecting children gathered around that big rough table."

Oma smiled and laid a hand on Maria's arm. "And now you yourself read from its pages to this half-blind old lady—and bring great comfort to her heart."

"What shall I read tonight?" Maria asked, knowing full well this might be her last opportunity.

Oma sighed, then smiled once more. "Ah, Maaike, my golden-haired child who has grown into the most beautiful of all healer ladies, can you find Psalm 56, I think it is verses 3 and 4? I have carried these words with me all my days, and tonight, almost more than at any other time, I need them with all my heart."

Maria opened the book and leafed through its pages, allowing her fingers to feel each page. It reminded her of the day she'd discovered her mother's herbal book and how she'd sought, by feeling the page with her fingers, to somehow find her mother. Tonight, she had the same sensation—seeking to find the comfort of God Himself in His holy pages. She found the spot Oma wanted and began to read aloud:

"When I am afraid . . ." she heard Oma speaking it with her. Together they went on, Maria reading, Oma reciting from the big book of her memory:

> *I will put my trust in Thee.*
> *In God whose word I praise,*
> *In God I have put my trust;*
> *I shall not be afraid.*

"Thank you, oh thank you, my Maaike," Oma said, her voice barely above a whisper.

Maria closed the book and laid it on the table. She and Oma embraced, dampening each other's shoulders with their tears, until Maria heard the clock tower chiming out into the night. It was time to let go.

"Oh, how I will miss you!" Oma grasped Maria's hand as if she would never let it go.

"And I shall miss you, Oma," Maria said. "I wish I did not have to go. But Emilie is staying. Eight years old, growing and learning, she'll bring you much sunshine. How I will miss her too. But I shall return soon."

"No, my child, it shall not be." Maria saw the tear-stained face in the candlelight and felt her heart break.

"You cannot know that," she protested.

"Ah, but I do," Oma said, resting her hand on hers without looking at her.

"Oma, how I hope you are mistaken. But whether you are or not, please promise me you will remember the four words you taught me. They have carried you through a life filled with disappointments and losses. Do not forget them now."

Oma bit her lip, nodded slightly, and stroked Maria's hand with her fingers. "Yes, I shall hold them tightly."

"Trust God with everything." They said it together.

"I shall try." Oma paused, then said, "Now, you must go. Goodnight, fair Maaike."

"Goodnight, my Oma."

They embraced once more, then Maria gently pulled free and walked softly out into a starlit night and to her Dillenburg room for the last time, whispering as she went, "When I am afraid . . . I will trust God with everything . . . Thank You, oh God, for such a grandmother!"

Historical Note:

On June 18, 1580, Juliana von Stolberg died in her own bed at the Dillenburg.

For months before she died, she had had one wish, to see her two sons once more. For reasons only God could know, that wish was denied her. But she had daughters nearby who visited her frequently. Sadly, none of her children were there at the moment of her passing. But she spent her last days peacefully, with a household of grandchildren and servants attending to her every need.

She died full of faith in Jesus Christ, still trusting Him to care for all of her ten children who still lived, along with their families—husbands and wives and the 168 grandchildren living when she died.

EPILOGUE

ANSWERED PRAYERS AND A LIVING MEMORIAL

JUNE 18, 1612 (*Journal Entry*)

BUREN

My heart goes round and round on this anniversary date of Oma's death. So much would I wish to tell my beloved Oma, if I could have but one more afternoon to sit with her on our well-worn pondering bench to share our hearts and souls . . . so much has happened . . . these things she would much want to know, and I would love to tell her:

My gentle Oma,
Thirty-two years ago, on this date, you passed from this life at the Dillenburg into your heavenly home with the Jesus you had loved and trusted all your days. How I wanted to be there to hold your hand and soothe your brow and to give you one final herbal tonic.

I would have wished to read to you again from Psalm 56. But God—and my father—had other plans. Afterwards,

I longed so to go with the crowd of people that accompanied you to your final resting place in the little church on the side of the hill. I've not been back in all these years. But I remember often visiting the site of Opa's burial there. So in my imagination, I go there often and I can clearly see your stone beside his.

Today is a special day in my life too. But first, I must tell you about some important things that have happened since you left. I think God may have let you see it all, but maybe not. So . . .

Will you come and sit beside me on our favorite pondering bench in the garden? In my mind's eye, I can see your beautiful face and hear your gentle breathing and tell you what has happened from then till now.

You know about my days with Father and Charlotte. They were difficult days. We lived in such poor circumstances, and the castle in Antwerp was dreadfully cold. But, in spite of all that, they were happy days. Charlotte proved to be just as she had seemed in her many loving letters. She showed me a beautiful new description for the word *stepmother*. She was indeed every bit as different from Mad Anna as anyone could hope for.

God gave Father and Charlotte six little girls in the seven years they were married. That big cold castle in Antwerp echoed and sometimes vibrated with the sounds of voices and footsteps. I can still see Charlotte sitting rosy-cheeked and glowing with admiration for her husband. Her lap was always filled with bouncing little girls and a pregnant belly, while her toe gently rocked the cradle. She looked for all the world like a contented queen on her throne.

And Father? Whenever he was at home, his eyes always sparkled, and smiles and laughter marked his every movement. Never had I seen him so relaxed and happy.

But then, King Philip issued a ban and spread it all over the Low Countries. It was unbelievable the things he said about my father. Charlotte and I saw the paper one time, attached to a tree. It read:

> I, King Philip of Spain, declare Willem van Oranje to be a wretched hypocrite, the chief author of all our troubles, a traitor and enemy of ourselves and our country . . . I empower all my subjects to seize the person and goods of this Willem van Oranje as enemy of the human race. To anyone who has the heart to free us of this pest, and who will deliver him alive or dead, or take his life, I hereby promise, on the word of a king, the sum of 25,000 crowns in gold.

Father, a traitor, a pest? It was awful, Oma. We all read it in grief and, from that moment on, we knew Father's day would come. And it did. Two times would-be assassins shot their bullets into him. The first time Charlotte hovered over him day and night until she made herself ill. In a short while, Father was healed and together they went to the church to give thanks.

But Charlotte's energies were used up. She and father returned to the castle, she to her bed. Within three days my beloved stepmother had died, leaving nine of us motherless and my father absolutely smitten with grief such as I have never seen. For once, I saw him cry.

Anna and I gathered around the little girls and did all we could to care for them, but we had not the wisdom, the strength, nor the mother-heart of Charlotte. Within a year

Father had married again—to another French woman. He said they were the best kind of women for him, and I think he expected Louise to be another Charlotte. To be sure, no one could meet those expectations, but Louise did well in her own way, and I believe Father loved her. And when she bore his next and final child, it was a son.

How we welcomed little Frederick Willem. Imagine the light in Father's eyes. He had another son, after all those girls! The boy has grown into a man who would make our father proud. In fact, I am sure he will one day follow in Father's steps as a leader of the Low Countries.

Finally, on the second assassination attempt, King Philip got his dearest wish. Oh, Oma! That was indeed the darkest day of our lives!

Our family lived then in a charming old former convent in the city of Delft, and I remember well the day a young Frenchman came to see Father. I was in the room at the time. A strange, dark man he was, with eyes that made me uncomfortable.

"I must return to my home in France," he said to Father. Pointing to his torn, shabby shoes, he added, "But as you can see, I am in need of a new pair of shoes. These will hardly take me there. Can you perhaps find a graciousness in your heart to lend me money to buy a pair for my journey?"

I did not trust him, but you know Father. Almost without hesitation, he gave the young man coins and sent him out to do his business. The next day, Father was descending the stairs, headed away from the dining hall after eating the noon meal, when two gunshots sounded and Father crumpled to the stairs. By the time his guards reached him, his breath was nearly gone. The powerful shots tore through his lungs and stomach and embedded themselves in the wall. I am told that you can still see the holes in the plaster, with stains of blood spattered all around.

When the guards caught the fleeing assassin trying to scale the fence, they recognized him. It was the Frenchman returned. With the money Father had given him to buy shoes, he had purchased a gun and come back to follow King Philip's orders to "rid the world of this pest." The guards hanged him in the city square before sundown that same day.

On that day, Oma, and for some time afterwards, I threw away the four words you had given me. "Trust God with everything!" How could I? I've since learned to live by those words again, but for a long time I remained angrier with God than I would like to tell you.

I went to the burial with my heart splintered into too many pieces to count. Hundreds of people from all over the country gathered to mourn the death of the man they now called Father Willem. He lies in the Great Church in Delft. On his tomb is a perfectly carved likeness of the man I loved more than any other on earth, with his little dog lying at his feet.

I wonder if the world will ever know how good and gracious your son Willem was, Oma. You taught him so well about fairness, justice, and kindness. And always he seemed to be opening doors for people who used his gifts to do him harm.

Just recently I learned another dreadful story of this kind. I know you remember that day when, at your urging, Father granted a pardon to Jan Rubens, Anna's lover. I'll never forget how overjoyed his wife, Marie Pippelinck, was, or how good I felt inside. Did you know, Oma, that later she bore Rubens a son who has become a famous painter? Pieter Paul Rubens is his name. He paints wonderful things, I've been told, though I've seen none of them.

The tragedy is that this man has become a champion of King Philip's cause. It is an irony. I understand he, among others, attempts to persuade our Maurits and the leaders of the Low Countries to give up their demands for freedom and be content to live forever as Spanish subjects.

I would like to find Rubens one day in his studio and remind him that he owes his existence to Willem van Oranje. Do you think he would care, Oma? Would it matter, even a little bit?

So much more I wanted to tell you about. You would also be proud of Maurits. He took Father's place as leader of the Resistance. He has never married, but has become a military man of great fame all over Europe. We never dreamed of such things when he was born, so scrawny and sickly and always crying, did we? Little Anna grew to be a fine young lady, though there was always a little bit of her mother in her. When she was twenty-four years old, she married a son of Onkel Jan. Then less than six months later she herself died. About fifteen years ago Emilie married a Portuguese prince, but I don't believe she is happy.

Oh, yes, you remember Christina Diez, that child of Jan Rubens that Mad Anna was pregnant with when they arrested her? Even before you died, Onkel Jan and his wife had taken her in to raise her. I find it ever so admirable that Onkel Jan has always taken the best care of her. He gave her a fine education, even found her a good husband. I understand she has nothing but kind words to say for your wonderful family, Oma. You taught them so well.

Three other things you would be happy to know.

On my thirty-ninth birthday, at last, I married. Father never had the time or the money to find me a husband. So on my own I chose Philips, Count of Hohenlo. His brother Wolfgang had already married your own daughter Magdalena. Philips had been one of Maurits's faithful soldiers for many years and did much to further the cause of the Low Countries. He was a bit wild. He drank a lot and had a terrible temper at times—life with him was not always easy. But he loved me and we had eleven good years together before he died.

Then, the year after I was married, joy of joys, Philips Willem came home from Spain. Ah, I could scarcely believe when I heard it. I only saw him once, though, and he was so changed, Oma. Twenty-eight years he was gone, held like a prisoner in a land he had not chosen. King Philip was good to him, but he poisoned his mind. My brother came home as fiercely loyal to King Philip as Maurits is to Father's cause.

But Philips Willem has no interest in running the government, and I am most happy to report that he loves our father still. If anyone dares to criticize our Father Willem, he will not hesitate to fight them on the spot. So yes, Oma, as you promised me, God did bring him back. I still wear that ruby necklace he gave me. Since Philips Willem returned in good health, it reminds me every day that God can be trusted after all.

Oh, yes, and I keep the little sprig of lavender you gave me on my first visit to your apotheek. It lies in a box with my writing papers, where it lends them its wonderful fragrance and reminds me of your gentle devotion and virtue.

This last thing, and then I go. For most of my life since Father died, I have lived here in my mother's old family home in Buren.

God has never given me children of my own, as He did to you. But all through my life I have found ways to help other people's children. Often I have thought about how you spent your life caring for and educating those noblemen's children in your school in the Dillenburg.

I have not the means to do such as that, but I have built here in this town of Buren a home for orphans. It opens its doors tomorrow with the rising of the sun. It is not so big as I would like it to be. But it is beautiful, bright, and cheerful—well staffed with young women with lots of mother-love to give. I plan to share my herb garden with the young women who prepare to be wives and mothers and run healthy households one day.

So you see, while I'm getting a late start here and will not live to run this orphanage as many years as you ran your school in the Dillenburg, it will stand as a living memorial to all you taught me. My dearest Oma, your legacy and your teaching will live on and on. Someday perhaps the whole world will know you as we knew you—Beloved Mother of us all—and believe as you taught us that you never kill a person for what he or she believes.

Your forever faithful and loving granddaughter, Maaike
Princess of Oranje, Countess of Buren

Historical Note: Maria died on October 10, 1616, at the age of 60 years.

Author's Note

Juliana von Stolberg and her granddaughter Maria were real people living in a real time, struggling with real problems. They lived more than four hundred years ago, and neither of them had any idea that they would be remembered past the lives of their children or grandchildren.

But Juliana became the great Queen Mother of the Netherlands. For centuries, the Dutch people have given her a special place of reverence in their hearts and literature. Even more important, Juliana's convictions set a whole new pattern for the western world.

I first met Juliana in a book of Dutch history borrowed from the library. Our family had spent three years in the Netherlands, during my husband's tour of military duty there. While living there, I learned from my grandmother that her grandfather Shriver (which means writer) had come from Holland, and I was curious to know what had happened in that country before we lived there.

In the history books, I read about Juliana von Stolberg and her son Willem van Oranje. He was the George Washington of Holland, who began a revolution that finally won that country its independence from Spain. Juliana captivated my heart.

I marveled at her ability to give birth to and raise seventeen children without anesthetics, antibiotics, disposable diapers, or prepared baby foods. At the same time, she oversaw the work of a large and complicated noble household. She also tended an herb garden and made herbal cures, which she administered to villagers and household members—family and servants alike. She and her husband founded and ran a school for noblemen's children. And after her husband died, Juliana ran the school herself for twenty years, until the year before she died at the age of seventy-four (a ripe old age in the sixteenth century).

But more, I was awestruck by this woman's strong courage in the face of incredible difficulties. She lost four of her five sons to the cause of freedom in the Low Countries (modern Holland, Belgium, and Luxemburg). Her faith, severely tested on every side, was absolutely unshakable.

The more I read, the more I wanted to know.

Then one day, I sat in the Royal Dutch Archives in The Hague, looking at old relics of this sixteenth-century family. I held in my hands a packet of old letters— written by Juliana von Stolberg. I examined the faded handwriting and ran my fingers over the sealing wax still attached. I shook my head and stood in absolute awe. And in that sacred moment, I felt with my heart—not just my head— that Juliana was a real, living woman, not just an entry in the history books. I had met her almost in person!

I came home from that trip determined to one day write Juliana's story so that people in this country could get to know this incredible woman. In her day, they called her "beloved mother of us all." When you finish reading her story, it will not surprise me if you call her that yourself.

In writing Juliana and Maria's story, I used all the important real events that happened and are recorded in the history books. But I have added specific details of how each thing took place, with the use of my imagination. Except for Toske, Pieter-Lucas, and the butcher's wife in the village, all the characters are also taken directly from history books. I tried to be totally true to the spirit and the record of the facts, while helping you to enter into the story and feel as if you are a part of it. This is what we call "biographical fiction."

After reading this book, I hope mothers and daughters will talk together about some of the following:

Ways that Juliana's world was different from ours.

- Ways that her world was really not all that different from ours.
- How Maria's view of God developed as she grew older. What were the things that shaped her relationship with God?
- How Juliana taught Maria.
- How people in the sixteenth century came to call themselves Christians.
- How Juliana treated her servants.
- The differences between the faithful, believing Juliana and the selfish, wayward Anna von Saxony.
- How Juliana's views about religious freedom affected the governments of the western world.
- How Maria managed to cope with what we today would call abandonment and an emotionally unstable lifestyle.
- Standards for purity and the consequences of disregarding them, as evidenced in Anna's life.
- Evidences of the faithfulness of God in protecting and caring for His people.
- How people of the sixteenth century thought about a "just war."

I hope and pray that you will find in Juliana von Stolberg and her granddaughter the kind of godly, real, and intimate friends I have found. I also pray that they will help you grow as women with all the courage and determination needed to let God use you to change your world.

Ethel Herr

GLOSSARY

apotheek: A pharmacy. The shop where medicinal and herbal cures were mixed and/or sold. A little box containing the medicines a healer lady was taking to her patients was also called an "apotheek."

Breda (Braid—AH): City in Holland, located on a broad place in the Ah River. Willem of Oranje inherited a castle home in this city from his cousin, and it became his home headquarters for many years.

convent in Delft: The lovely old building still stands in the city of Delft. It has become a museum. If you go there to visit, you can still see the blood-stained holes in the wall.

the Dillenburg: The Castle on the Dill. Name for the castle where Juliana lived. Two parts of the word explain its meaning:

> **burg**: German word for castle.

> **dill**: River Dill that ran by the foot of the hill where the castle was located.

It was built on a high hill as a fortified building to protect the inhabitants from their warlike enemies. It consisted of a collection of many buildings clustered around a central courtyard. These were enclosed inside a high wall. Down below, a rock wall also fenced off the entire hill. The castle was destroyed by the French in the eighteenth century, but some ruins (including parts of the rock fence and all of the chapel on the side of the hill) remain today for visitors to explore.

herbal recipes in this book: All the recipes you find here were copied from an old seventeenth-century herbal book, and I have used the same spelling as I found there, which is often different from ours. The name of the book is *The Herbal of General History of Plants*, by John Gerard, published in England in 1633. It was a compilation of several herbal books from Juliana's time and before, along with a few of Mr. Gerard's own additions.

humors: In days before the discovery of germs, practitioners of the medical arts believed that something called "humors" lived in the body and could make one either well or sick. They most often used potions concocted from herbs to drive out the bad humors and restore the patient to health.

Jan (Yawn): same as "John."

linden tree: Today there is a special linden tree still in place at the Dillenburg. It has a marker to tell you that here, in 1568, Willem van Oranje met with the leaders of the Low Countries to plan the war of revolt against Spain.

Maaike (Maa-EE-kuh): Nickname for Maria. History records that her family in the Dillenburg all called her by this name. It was a sign of their affection for her.

madness of Anna: In the sixteenth century, the word "mad" did not mean simply "angry," as we use it today. "Mad" described anyone with wild and uncontrollable behavior. Anna was possibly mentally ill, or an alcoholic, or simply a young woman who refused to discipline herself and got out of control.

In Anna's day, madness often was thought to be caused by demonic influences. Mad people were sometimes tried and convicted as witches and either imprisoned for life or executed.

Sadly, it is possible that at least some of the ills that were called madness in the sixteenth century could have been cured with the right herbal medicines, had they been better understood at the time. Juliana and other herbalists searched for cures, but the secrets waited to be revealed to scientists in a later time.

Oma/Opa: Grandma and Grandpa in both German and Dutch.

Onkel (Ohn-cul): German for uncle.

phlegm: Term used for the common cold.

religious freedom: In the sixteenth century, the religion of the king was, by law, the religion of all his subjects. But following the invention of the printing press, new ideas began to circulate, along with Bibles in the language of the people.

Many wars broke out as a result, because the new ideas gave people a desire to worship as they thought the Bible taught them to worship.

In the midst of the chaos, Juliana von Stolberg was teaching her sons an idea totally new for their day: You must never kill a man, woman, or child because of what they believe.

In the Low Countries, her sons led a resistance against the King of Spain who refused to grant the citizens freedom of worship. The war lasted for eighty years.

Later, when a group of Christians from England fled to the Low Countries from religious persecution, they lived there (in the city of Leyden) for twenty years. There they learned the ways of religious freedom. When they finally came to the wild lands of America, they brought those ideas with them, and they eventually were built into our constitution.

rheumy: Congested, as in having a cold.

Tante (TAWN-tuh): Dutch word for aunt.

Timeline

The Life of Juliana von Stolberg and Maria van Buren

1487   April 10, Willem von Nassau (Juliana's second husband) is born.

1506   February 15, Juliana von Stolberg is born.

1517   Juliana moves to Konigstein to live with aunt and uncle in the summer.

   October 31, Martin Luther nails his 95 Theses to Wittenberg door.

1523   June 9, Juliana marries Philips II von Hanau.

1529   March 28, Juliana's husband, Phillips II von Hanau, dies.

1531   September 30, Juliana von Stolberg marries Willem von Nassau.

1533   April 24, Willem van Oranje born to Juliana and Willem von Nassau.

1544   Willem van Oranje goes to Brussels to live in court of Charles V in June.

1551   July 8, Willem van Oranje marries Anne van Buren.

1554   December 19, Philips Willem born to Willem and Anne.

1556   February 7, Maria born to Willem and Anne.

1558   March 24, Anne van Buren dies.

1559	October 6, Willem von Nassau (Juliana van Stolberg's second husband) dies.
1561	August 24, Willem van Oranje (Juliana's son) marries Anna von Saxony.
1567	Willem van Oranje and family flee to Dillenburg in April.
1568	February 13, Philips Willem (Maria's brother) kidnapped and taken to Spain.
	May 23, Adolph von Nassau (Juliana's son) killed in first major battle of the war for independence in the Low Countries.
1568	Anna von Saxony leaves Dillenburg, returns, gets pregnant, leaves again, summer–fall.
1569	April 10, Emilie van Nassau born to Anna von Saxony in another city and sent back to Juliana to be raised.
1571	Anna von Saxony and Jan Rubens imprisoned for adultery in the spring. Willem van Oranje divorces Anna.
1574	April 14, Ludwig von Nassau and Hendrik von Nassau (Juliana's sons) killed in battle.
1575	July 12, Willem van Oranje marries Charlotte de Bourbon.
1577	Maria goes to live with her father and Charlotte in the summer.
	December 18, Anna von Saxony dies, insane, in a dungeon.
1580	June 18, Juliana von Stolberg dies.
1582	May 5, Charlotte de Bourbon dies.
1583	April 13, Willem van Oranje marries Louise de Coligny.
1584	July 10, Willem van Oranje is assassinated.
1595	February 7, Maria marries Philips Count of Hohenlo.
1596	February 11, Philips Willem (Maria's brother) returns from Spain.
1606	March 6, Maria's husband, Philips van Hohenlo, dies.
1612	June 18, Maria opens an orphanage.
1616	October 10, Maria dies at 60 years of age.

BIBLIOGRAPHY

Alexander, J. H. *Ladies of the Reformation.* Harpenden, Herts, England: Gospel Standard Strict Baptist Trust, 1978.

Collins, Marie and Virginia Davis. *A Medieval Book of Seasons.* New York: Harper Collins, 1992.

Cushman, Karen. *The Midwife's Apprentice.* New York: Clarion Books, 1995. A Newberry Medal Award winner.

Douglas, J. D., ed. *Dictionary of the Christian Church.* Grand Rapids: Zondervan, 1978.

Gerard, John. *The Herbal or General History of Plants* (the complete 1633 edition as revised and enlarged by Thomas Johnson). New York: Dover Books, 1975.

Halliday, Sonia and Laura Lushington. *Stained Glass.* New York: Crown Publishers, 1976.

Herr, Ethel. *The Dove and the Rose.* Minneapolis: Bethany House, 1996.

———. *The Maiden's Sword.* Minneapolis: Bethany House, 1997.

———. *The Citadel and the Lamb.* Minneapolis: Bethany House, 1998. (Ethel Herr's books, The Seeker Series, are novels about Willem van Oranje and his mother, Juliana von Stolberg.)

Poortvliet, Rien. *Daily Life In Holland in 1566.* New York: Harry N. Abrams, 1992 (English translation).

Wedgwood, C. V. *William the Silent.* New York: W. W. Norton, 1944. First published in U.S. 1968.

Ethel Herr is an accomplished author, speaker, teacher, and historian. She has written more than ten books, including The Seekers series of historical fiction. Ethel has also written many articles, short stories, and poems. She teaches writing, research, the arts, and the Bible to all ages.

Ethel is a historian specializing in sixteenth-century Europe— the arts, herbalism, socio-religious conflict, and Christianity. She is associated with the history department at Multnomah Bible College, which awards an annual Ethel Herr Prize in History.

Ethel lives in California with her husband. They have three grown children and five grandchildren.